A Pandemic of Lunacy

≈

LIBERTY & FREEDOM UNDER SIEGE

William James Moore

i

"Knowledge will forever govern ignorance, and a people who mean to be their own Governors, must arm themselves with the power knowledge gives." — James Madison (1751 – 1836)

"To sit back hoping that someday, someway, someone will make things right is to go on feeding the crocodile, hoping he will eat you last – but eat you he will." — Ronald Reagan (1911-2004)

"It does not require a majority to prevail, but rather an irate, tireless minority keen to set brush fires in people's minds." — Samuel Adams (1722-1803)

"All that is necessary for the triumph of evil is for good men [and women] to do nothing." — Edmund Burke (1729-1797)

"Our lives begin to end the day we become silent about things that matter." — Plato (428/427 or 424/423BC – 348/347 BC)

= = =

Dedication

To our grandson Matthew "Matt"

May Matthew and other U.S. citizen recipients of our nation's many priceless opportunities, demanding responsibilities, and awesome challenges, . . . be blessed with the means, desire, and commitment to experience, enjoy, respect, protect, and pass on to future generations, an America of inalienable (God-given) Rights to life, liberty, and pursuit of happiness.

"In the beginning God created the heaven and the earth."
— Genesis 1:1

"The Serenity Prayer"

*"**God** grant me the . . .*
__Serenity__ to accept the things I cannot change;
__Courage__ to change the things I can; and
__Wisdom__ to know the difference."

— Reinhold Niebuhr (1892–1971)

= = =

"Learn from yesterday, live for today, hope for tomorrow.   The important thing is not to stop questioning." — Albert Einstein (1879-1955)

"Extremes to the right and to the left of any political dispute are always wrong." — Dwight D. Eisenhower (1890-1969)

"Let us not seek the Republican answer or the Democratic answer, but the right answer. Let us not seek to fix the blame for the past. Let us accept our own responsibility for the future." — John F. Kennedy (1917-1963)

"Those who stand for nothing fall for anything." — Alexander Hamilton (1757-1804)

"The foundation of every state is the education of its youth."
                                                — Diogenes (412BC-323BC)

Contents

Contents (Continued)

In Remembrance of
Our Mothers and Fathers

To my mother Hazel, Ann's mother Lillie, my natural father James, Ann's natural father Robert, Ann's stepfather George, and my stepfathers Ernest and Marvin. Each, a once young child with curiosity, awe, plans, and dreams. Born into daunting economic circumstances of the Great Depression (the deepest, longest-lasting, and most wide-spread economic depression of the 20th Century) — involving severe economic circumstances far beyond any true understanding of we later generations. Like so many others of that time, each, along with their families, often faced with life-consuming focus on basic survival. Challenged by limited education and scarce, often extremely- hazardous and physically-demanding work environments. A world where attitudes of being "owed, deserving, entitled, and a victim" had no welcome or relevance. With the "how to" as spouses, parents, and grandparents, derived from learn-as-you-go and the school of often harsh challenges. Their respective strengths, weaknesses, failures, and successes, not always equally recognized, understood, shared, or otherwise experienced within family. Each an enviable example of giving and self-sacrifice. Loving parents who did and gave their best. Leaving a legacy of vital life-lessons, treasured experiences, and cherished memories. So deeply and dearly loved by so many — and now longed for and missed beyond words. ♥

Special Appreciation

To my wife Ann, daughter Jamie, son Ryan, grandson Matthew, and Mike H. And to other "Family"—all with whom we have been, and may yet be, privileged to share treasured relationships and priceless memories.

= = =

"A family is a bunch of people who keep confusing you with someone you were as a kid." — Robert Brault

"I know why families were created with all their imperfections. They humanize you. They are made to make you forget yourself occasionally, so that the beautiful balance of life is not destroyed."
— Anais Nin

"Children begin by loving their parents; as they grow older they judge them; sometimes they forgive them." — Oscar Wilde

"We all have our strengths and our failings. — Hannah Simone

"Enjoy the little things, for one day you may look back and realize they were the big things." — Robert Brault

"Sometimes you will never know the value of a moment until it becomes a memory." — Dr. Seuss

"Other things may change us, but we start and end with family."
— Anthony Brandt

Recognition

In supplement to my personal life experiences, observations, and views, the content of this writing was also drawn from that of many known and unknown others. All to whom I express sincere appreciation for the enlightenment shared and access to crucial information.

= = =

"As we express our gratitude, we must never forget that the highest appreciation is not to utter words, but to live by them."
— *John F. Kennedy (1917-1963)*

"Those who expect to reap the blessings of freedom, must, like men, undergo the fatigue of supporting it." —*Thomas Paine (1737-1809)*

"Government exists to protect us from each other. Where government has gone beyond its limits is in deciding to protect us from ourselves." — *Ronald Reagan (1911-2004)*

"The welfare of our country is the great object to which our cares and efforts ought to be directed." — *George Washington (1732-1799)*

"We hold these truths to be self-Evident, that all men are created equal, that they are endowed by their Creator with certain unalienable Rights that among these are **Life, Liberty and the pursuit of Happiness**. ---That to secure these rights, Governments are instituted among Men, deriving their just powers from the consent of the governed,"

— *The U.S. Declaration of Independence, 1776*

Introduction

> *"Freedom is a fragile thing and is never more than one generation away from extinction—it is not ours by inheritance; it must be fought for and defended constantly by each generation, for it comes only once to a people. Those who have known freedom and then lost it have never known it again."* — Ronald Reagan (1911-2004), 40th U.S. President.
>
> *"Liberty may be endangered by the abuse of liberty, but also by the abuse of power."* — James Madison (1751-1836), 4th U.S. President; one of U.S. Founding Fathers; hailed as the "Father of the U.S. Constitution."

Dear Reader,

As breathtaking fireworks displays and other spectacular celebrations around the globe marked the arrival of the New Year 2019, the Earth's human population surpassed an estimated 7.6 billion (7,600,000,000). With about 1.4 billion being in China; 1.3 billion in India; .3 billion in the U.S.; .1 billion in Russia; and the remaining 4.5 billion elsewhere.

Although most efforts to get a mental grasp of "7.6 billion" of anything are likely most futile, nevertheless, consider for a moment . . . if the adults and teenagers alone within the afore noted global population could, with arms stretched outward from their sides, join one another's hands—the total length of the resulting "human line" would, roughly speaking, wrap around the Earth at least 228 times.

However, the arrival of 2019—of yet another year—did not represent a time for celebration for all.

For, shamefully, various reports still showed—even after thousands of years of human struggle—only about 39 percent to be "**Free**," 24 percent to be "**Partly Free**," and 37 percent to be "**Not Free**." With the "basic elements of freedom" addressed by such reports considered to include: guaranteed free and fair elections; rights of minorities; freedom of the press; and rule of law.

The arrival of 2019 also marked another notable statistic— some 13 consecutive years of decline in global freedom. Following, for example, the horrific 2017 campaign of ethnic cleansing in Myanmar (formally Burma) in Southeast Asia, and the continuing slide of Turkey and Hungary into authoritarian rule, etc.

Not to mention, the ancient-rooted evils of radical-militant Islam that continue to wage war against 21st century civilization. Or, a seemingly endless civil war in Syria that, since its beginning in 2011, had by 2019 killed and estimated

400,000 Syrians and caused more than 5.6 million to flee the country.

And, as liberty and freedom unrelentingly struggle against widespread age-old attacks — the United States, United Kingdom, Germany, and the world's other most powerful democracies, continue to be mired in social and economic turmoil and political partisan fragmentation.

Consequences magnified in large measure by an overwhelming influx of refugees and invasion of illegal aliens. All of which further complicating the long-standing struggle of liberty and freedom against global extinction. A battle for survival made even more worrisome by another most unsettling reality.

That being, we now have several younger generations who have little to no memory of, or demonstrated concern about, the world's long struggles against fascism and communism. Nor, do such generations reveal anything resembling a survival-crucial grasp, of the truly serious threats to liberty and freedom still posed by such tyrannical ideologies.

While certainly not alone, the U.S. now has more and more people who have no idea, for example, who Stalin, Hitler, and Mao Zedong (Wade-Giles Romanization, Mao Tse-tung) were. Or that each came to power preaching the same socialist-rooted promises as now being pushed by much of the radical-left. Or that socialism is history's time and again proven "stepping stone" to communism.

While threats to liberty and freedom come in many forms and with many faces, all are driven by overwhelming greed; lust for power, dominance, and control; and other unrestrained self-serving behavior. Each feeding off of and hence being enabled by a blend of self-destructive ignorance, apathy, complacency, denial, greed, and counter-productive fears of not only the targets of oppression—but also of others who turn their heads in detachment from the plight of others.

None the least of the many 21st century threats to liberty and freedom, is a "**Pandemic of Lunacy**" rampantly spreading throughout much of the World today. A lunacy not only being a most serious threat to the thus far fortunate now living in the U.S. and various other so-called free societies. But also posing a hope-destroying threat to the dreams of millions worldwide now living under tyranny or other oppression.

Chief among the symptoms of this truly sinister pandemic, is a chronic inability or refusal to distinguish fantasy from reality and/or falsehoods and distortions from truth and fact. A nature of lunacy further leaving the infected with a dangerous absence of rational thought and a growing inability to control impulsive, and often destructive, behavior.

Examples of existence and consequences of this menacing threat are many, varied, and growing in number. Some, certainly not all, are identified through somewhat random and intentionally briefed essays within this book. Each tailored for consideration by open, reality-accepting, and otherwise rational minds.

It is the hope and aim of this writing, to in some way help ensure that where liberty and freedom now exist, such continue to thrive, and where now denied, will one day soon be gained and secured. That something within these pages be of meaningful encouragement and support to those committed to doing what each we can toward such aims. And in doing so, that one and all find the strength and means to never be silenced, intimidated, or otherwise hindered by those striving to deny of others the inalienable (God-given) rights to life, liberty, and pursuit of happiness.

— William James Moore

= = =

"Whoever would overthrow the liberty of a nation must begin by subduing the freeness of speech." — *Benjamin Franklin (1706-1790), author, scientist, inventor, diplomat, one of U.S. Founding Fathers.*

*"It was by the sober sense of our citizens that we were safely and steadily conducted **from monarchy** to republicanism, and it is by the same agency alone we can be kept from falling back."* — *Thomas Jefferson (1723-1826), 3rd U.S. President; one of U.S. Founding Fathers.*

"I am only one, but still I am one. I cannot do everything, but still I can do something; and because I cannot do everything, I will not refuse to do something that I can do." — Helen Keller (1880-1968), American author, political activist and lecturer, and first deafblind person to earn a Bachelor of Arts degree.

Liberty & Freedom

> *"America will never be destroyed from the outside. If we falter and lose our freedoms, it will be because we destroyed ourselves.* —Abraham Lincoln (1809–1865), 16th U.S. President.*
>
> *"The price of freedom is eternal vigilance." —Thomas Jefferson (1773-1826), 3rd U.S. President and a U.S. Founding Father.*

Liberty and **Freedom** are of course terms that can, as applicable, be interchangeable or considered distinct. And in the minds of many can also have various meanings. Therefore, and given that both terms are vital elements of the primary focus of this book, an upfront explanation of their usage within this writing is considered all-important.

Generally speaking, while both terms refer to the quality or state **of** being **free**—"**Liberty**" usually means to be **free to do** something. For example, the **Liberty** to carry out freedom of expression, speech, assembly, religion, and the press. As well as freedom to bear arms, pursue happiness, own property, and to act in fulfillment of one's potential, etc.

Whereas **"Freedom"** usually means to be **free from** something. For example, **freedom** from, tyranny, wrongful imprisonment, oppression, religious persecution, and unlawful search and seizure, etc.

Of course it is not realistic to think of **liberty** and **freedom** existing without **limitations**, since all aspects of life involve some nature of constraints. Such as, limited hours in a day, lifespan, income, reproductive years, length of seasons, physical strength, mental attributes, natural resources, etc.

And of course the activities of government are also subject to various limitations. For example, the U.S. Constitution includes many expressed and implied limitations on government and on those governed by it. The very word "govern" implies imposed limitations.

However, it seems especially noteworthy that when encountering limitations imposed by nature (e.g., effects of gravity, the weather, etc.), we don't typically feel all that personally offended, imposed upon, or taken advantage of. Nor, do we usually march in protest, revolt, etc., as a result of such constraints. To the contrary, we typically just focus on ways and means of dealing with nature's many realities.

However, the real rub comes from constraints created or imposed by government or other people. When, for example, we are seriously intimidated, forced to obey, abused, over-taxed, or over-regulated, etc. Or, when our freedom of speech, religion, privacy, property ownership, etc., are infringed upon. Or, when our right to bear arms or to pursue happiness are jeopardized.

Given the many intolerable constraints suffered at the hands of the British government, our country's founders had a very clear, up close, and personal understanding of what **liberty** and **freedom** meant—and what the absence of such entailed! And they had a very profound and experienced grasp of the fact that without both liberty and freedom, neither can exist.

In 1776 the U.S. Declaration of Independence from Britain stated in part: *"We hold these truths to be self-Evident, that all men are created equal, that they are endowed by their Creator with certain unalienable Rights that among these are Life, Liberty and the pursuit of Happiness. ---That to secure these rights, Governments are instituted among Men, deriving their just powers from the consent of the governed . . ."*

By 1789 our U.S. Constitution was ratified, but many of the founding fathers still had a very fresh memory of the tyranny and violations of human and civil rights earlier imposed by Britain. They also had very deep concerns about the potential tyranny that can result from a **strong central government**.

As a result they worked hard for a **bill of rights** specifically aimed at protecting the liberty/freedom of **we the people**. From their efforts and wisdom the first ten amendments to our Constitution—known as the **Bill of Rights**—were ratified on 15 December 1791.

Ever since our country's hard-fought-for beginning, countless people from near and far have continued to seek the special liberty and freedom offered by this great nation—this first and one-of-its-kind Constitutional Republic!

However, regardless of how defined, there will likely always exist differing views and attitudes about what liberty and freedom stand for. And, unfortunately, there will also likely always be those who, through ignorance or intent, behave as if such terms mean *"liberty and freedom to do whatever one wishes."* Nevertheless, and most fortunately, most of the more rational and considerate among us still seem to understand and generally demonstrate otherwise. By striving to apply, protect, and preserve liberty and freedom as more aptly meaning: *"unopposed to do whatever we want, but within limits that protect the equal liberty and freedom of others."*

Or, as paraphrased from the writings of Thomas Jefferson (1773-1826), 3rd U.S. President and a U.S. Founding Father— *"Rightful liberties and freedoms are unobstructed actions according to our respective individual will, within limits drawn around us by the equal rights of others."*

While never absent from our awareness that no liberty or freedom is absolute, or without restraint, nor immune from the every present threat of potential loss.

= = =

"Freedom is never more than one generation away from extinction." — *Ronald Reagan (1911-2004), 40th U.S. President.*

The U.S. National Debt:
"An Epitome of Lunacy"

> *"I place economy among the first and most important virtues, and public debt as the greatest of dangers to be feared...To preserve our independence, we must not let our rulers load us with perpetual debt. . .We must make our choice between economy and liberty or profusion and servitude. . ."* — *Thomas Jefferson (1743–1826)*

An "epitome" is of course commonly defined as a "perfect example." And it is therefore very likely that one would need to look long and hard to find a better example of lunacy than the "U.S. National Debt"!

For example, if you were a U.S. citizen at the beginning of 2019, **"your share"** of our (at that time) rapidly-approaching $22 trillion National Debt was over $67,000.00. Or, more than $179,000.00 if a U.S. taxpayer. And, **"your share"** of our federal government's (at that time) more than $122 trillion of Unfunded Liabilities (i.e., unfunded obligations [debt] to Social Security, Medicare, Veterans Benefits, etc.) was well over an additional $1 million. Totaling some $144 trillion (about **$1,179,000.00 per taxpayer**).

Indisputably, a mindboggling National Debt that has since reached and surpassed an even further inconceivable $22 trillion! A shameful liberty/freedom threatening legacy being passed on to the shoulders and backs of America's children, grandchildren, and generations not yet born.

But relax, there is no need for worry! Because, shared below is a simple, painless, and obvious solution:

(1.) Legitimate U.S. citizens should try hard to NEVER vote in any future U.S. elections;

(2.) However, if vote one must, then without fail always support: open borders; uncontrolled immigration; and "FREE" housing, food, clothing, medical care, income-inequality cash allowances, smartphones, college education, transportation, child care, legal counsel, and entertainment, taxpayer-funded subsidies for "climate change" rip-offs, etc., for everyone the radical-liberal political-left defines as being a "victim" or otherwise "in need"; and,

(3.) Strictly on an optional basis, consider some very serious prayers for present and future generations of Americans, just in case Steps (1.) and (2.) don't work out so well for some unforeseen reason.

Of course those yet hanging on to some resemblance of sanity will recognize that a "touch of satire" was used in the above so-called solution. With the hope of drawing special attention to a most serious liberty and freedom threatening concern— "our" U.S. National Debt. To what is truly an **epitome of lunacy**!

Historically speaking, a National Debt has been a part of our country since its beginning. The earliest record of such was prepared by Alexander Hamilton, the first U.S. Treasury Secretary and self-taught economist. Following the Revolutionary War, his 1790 analysis showed our National Debt to be about $75 million. A debt thereafter fueled over the centuries by additional wars, and by other circumstances driving government spending well beyond the funds it takes in.

Fast-forwarding about 216 years later to 1906, the year my dad was born, our National Debt was a little more than $2 billion. When my wife and I entered the world it had increased to $201 billion.

Around arrival of our two children it was about $427 billion, and by 1981 had reached $1 trillion. By 2003, the year we were blessed with our (the World's best-ever) grandson, it had jumped to $6.7 trillion, and by 2008 had climbed to more than $10 trillion. **And in February 2019, reached and surpassed $22 trillion—less than one year after hitting $21 trillion for the first time!**

Our **U.S. National Debt** is managed by the U.S. Treasury Department through its Bureau of the Public Debt, and made up of the combination of the following two broad categories:

(1.) **Public Deb**t: This is money our federal government borrows from American investors; foreign investors; foreign governments; etc., through the sale of U.S. Treasury Bills, Notes, and Bonds; U.S. Savings Bonds; etc. *In 2018, for example, this Public Debt portion amounted to about $15.8 trillion (about 75 percent of the total National Debt).*

(2.) Intra-governmental Debt: This is money our federal government owes itself. Such as money borrowed from the Social Security and Medicare trust funds; Military Retirement funds; Civil Service funds; Federal Reserve Banks; etc. *In 2018, for example, this Intra-governmental Debt portion amounted to about $5.2 trillion (about 25 percent of the total National Debt).*

Again, by the arrival of 2019 our (at that time) rapidly approaching **$22 trillion National Debt** had reached about:
- $67,000 for every U.S. citizen, or
- Over $179,000 for every U.S. taxpayer, or
- Over 6 times the yearly Federal Government tax revenues

Furthermore, as of this 2019 writing, with the exception of 2015, our National Debt has also "exceeded" our nation's Gross Domestic Product (GDP) since 2014, i.e., the total value of all goods and services produced in the U.S. for a given year.

And, as shown in the Chart below, prior to above noted unsettling trend, the last time our National Debt was "more than" our GDP was during the 1945–1947 time frame, when paying for World War II.

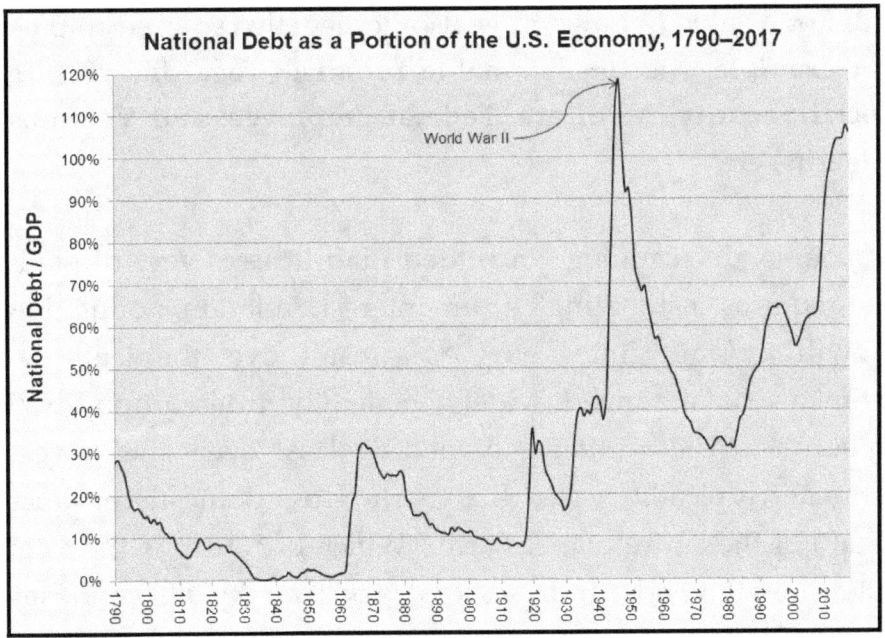

Now, a few words about the real "elephant in the room" — **Unfunded Liabilities**.

As staggering as a 2019 **$22 trillion** debt figure truly is, it makes up only part of our federal government's then total debt obligation. That is, only the **legally binding** portion. It doesn't include other amounts, such as the federal government's **Unfunded Liabilities**.

An **Unfunded Liability** is basically the amount, at any given time, by which future payment obligations exceed the present and forecasted value of the funds available to pay those obligations. In other words, the amount of money the government has "promised" to people, but in all likelihood will not be able to pay and is also not legally required to pay. **For example, the unsustainable promises regarding future Social Security, Medicare, Federal Employee, and Veterans benefits, etc**.

Of course, determining **Unfunded Liabilities** is very difficult and requires "estimating" future interest, inflation, population growth, mortality rates, etc. As a result, over the years the estimates have ranged widely; generally from around $80 trillion to $200 trillion. None the less, even the lowest estimates typically exceed the yearly gross domestic product (GDP) of the entire planet Earth. Which of course is the total value of all goods and services produced by all countries worldwide during a given year.

For example, the global GDP for 2019 was projected to be about $88.0 trillion. Whereas, for example, in March of 2019 our **U.S. Federal Government's actual "Unfunded Liabilities"** had surpassed **$122.9 trillion** — amounting to more than:

- **$373,000** for every U.S. citizen, or
- **$1,000,000** for every U.S. taxpayer.

It is also alarmingly noteworthy, that the biggest share of the above referenced **Unfunded Liabilities** consist of not-backed-up promises to future recipients of Social Security, Medicare and Veterans benefits.

Truly our federal government's **Unfunded Liabilities** are the **"elephant in the room"** no one wants to talk about! Least of all, those among us who continue to demand more and more so-called "free stuff." And the politicians who are willing to feed such out-of-control greed with unsustainable promises financed by more and more debt. Debt that "we the people" are ultimately accountable for. Debt that is being passed on to future generations of Americans to deal with and suffer the ultimate consequences of.

But, unfortunately there is even more! Our $22 trillion National Debt number in 2019 also does not include certain so-called "Agency Debt." That is, the amount of outstanding debt issued by various Federal Agencies, such as, the Federal Home Loan Bank (FHLB) and the "Ginnie Mae" – Government National Mortgage Association (GNMA), as well as government-sponsored enterprises, such as Fannie Mae and Freddie Mac.

Historically, Agency Debt has not been included in the total U.S. National Debt as published by the U.S. Department of the Treasury. And, what would be the size of this yet another "elephant in the room"? Well, for example, the Fiscal Year 2017, "Agency Debt" was reportedly about **$8.86 trillion**; and in Fiscal Year 2018 was projected to increase to about **$9.26 trillion**.

Never the less, whether our nation's obligations are reported as the **U.S. National Debt**, or the unsupported promises entailed in our **U.S. Unfunded Liabilities**, or so-called **Agency Debt**, all are in fact **"debt obligations"** that cannot be just wished or ignored away.

For, along with the many other realities of life, there "will be" a day of reckoning on this subject. The time when those from whom money has been borrowed, and those to whom money and benefits related promises have been made, will expect and demand fulfillment of those obligations. Regardless of the consequences; regardless of how painful or widespread the sacrifice and suffering.

As noted in the quotation at the beginning of this Section, Thomas Jefferson (1743–1826) considered the **"public debt"** to be the **"greatest danger to our independence."** His being a highly-qualified and not-to-taken-lightly view, considering that Jefferson was one of our country's Founding Fathers; the principal author of our Declaration of Independence in 1776; our third U.S. President; a passionate spokesman for democracy; our first U.S. Secretary of State under President Washington; organizer of the Democratic-Republican Party; and with worldwide influence, supported the rights of the individual.

Earlier in this Section it was noted that, historically speaking, a national debt has been a part of our country since its beginning. However, what has not been a part of our great nation until recent years is, for example, a nation being ravaged by "political correctness" — which, simply defined, is "denial of truth and reality." And, a nation more and more divided into groups that see themselves as "the victims," and groups that are being viewed and treated as "the oppressors." With "the victims" behaving like they are "owed" food, shelter, healthcare, entertainment, and every other want and need they identify. And, "the oppressors" of course being anyone not in agreement with the views and demands of "the victims."

Furthermore, what has also not always been a part of our once much prouder and more responsible nation, is a federal government of ever-growing magnitude (re: the example "Eight-Page List of Federal Government Agencies" included on pages 159-166). And, what has also not always been so widespread and nation destructively engrained, is the extent of voters willing to selfishly vote themselves unjustified benefits from the public treasury, and, politicians willing to selfishly use the public treasury to bribe voters in order to achieve or retain their positions of political power and personal gain.

And, our nation's history has not until more recent years included giving countless and often untraceable millions of illegal aliens access to our public treasury by way of housing, food stamps, healthcare, and other benefits—paid for by an America already in unsustainable debt.

Of course the above examples are but a snapshot few of a growing many of the contributors to a national debt of a magnitude that defies comprehension. For, it is highly likely that none among us can truly grasp the size of **"one trillion" (1,000,000,000,000)** of anything . . . let alone **"twenty-one trillion"**! Even with the aid of the many professionally-developed charts and graphic examples available through a growing number of web-sites, books, and other sources.

However, until choosing to benefit from such material, the following relatively simplified examples should serve as meaningful eye-openers to the truly staggering nature of a **$22 trillion** debt.

(1.) **$22 Trillion Dollars = $22,000,000,000,000 (or 22 million million)**.

(2.) The circumference of (distance around) the Earth is about **24,901** miles. A U.S. one dollar bill is 6.14 inches long. Lining up **22 trillion U.S. one dollar bills** lengthways would circle the Earth about **85,616** times.

(3.) A round-trip from the Earth to the planet Saturn and back would be about **1.66 billion miles**. Lining up **22 trillion U.S. one dollar bills lengthways** would reach more than **2.13 billion miles,** or well beyond a round trip from the Earth to Saturn and back.

(4.) With a volume of more than **472 million cubic feet**, the Boeing Everett factory in the state of Washington is reportedly the world's largest building. About **877.2 million cubic feet of space** would be needed to store **$22 trillion** — or a building about **1.85 times the size** of Boeing's huge facility.

(5.) To pay back **$22 trillion**, at a rate of one dollar per second, would take about **697,615 years**.

(6.) For a shameful period of time, "we" (through our federal government) have been **overspending** about **$1 trillion** in **new debt** each year. If a "very generous" taxpayer earning about $50,000 per year decided to use "all" of his or her income — to pay-off just the principal (not including interest) of one year of **new debt** — it would take **20 million years** to do so. Paying-off just the principal of our **total debt of $22 trillion** would take **440 million years**.

(7.) However, if a $22 trillion National Debt were to be divided between all income taxpayers — such as the 122 million or so estimated to exist in 2019 — then the principal of a $22 trillion debt could be wiped out in about **3.6 years**. But, this of course again assumes each income taxpayer earning about $50,000 per year. And, using "all" of their income for payment of this debt, and spending nothing on anything else, including food, shelter, clothing, transportation, healthcare, or entertainment, etc.!

Now, with the above examples freshly in mind, try as you may to mentally grasp the massive size of the "real elephant in the room"—our as of 2019 **U.S. Unfunded Liabilities totaling some $122 trillion!**

Naturally, by the time this book is published, many if not most of the numerical values stated herein will have changed. In some cases, very likely significantly so. As is well beyond extremely likely, our **U.S. National Debt** and **Unfunded Liabilities** will continue to grow and pose more and more threat—hastening the day of reckoning.

And such will be the case, regardless of how deep we bury our heads in apathy, complacency, denial, greed, counter-productive fears. In self-destructive behaviors driven in large measure a seemingly impossible-to-satisfy greed and demand **"to have it all now"**—regardless of the consequences. Regardless of the risk not only to present generations of Americans, but also more shamefully to the not yet born—those without a voice or other means to protect themselves from the past and present so-called adults in the room!

= = =

"The American Republic will endure until the day Congress discovers that it can bribe the public with the public's money."
                                    –Alexis De Tocqueville (1805-1859)

"There are two ways to enslave a nation. One is by the sword. The other is by debt." – John Adams (1735-1826), 2nd U.S. President.

"The trouble with Socialism is that eventually you run out of other people's money." – Margaret Thatcher (1925-2013), Prime Minister of the United Kingdom from 1979-1990

Where Do You & I Stand?

> "To sit back hoping that someday, someway, someone will make things right is to go on feeding the crocodile, hoping he will eat you last – but eat you he will."   – Ronald Reagan (1911-2004), 40th U.S. President

Although intentionally-limited in scope and detail, the previous Section should leave any rational person with a new or renewed awareness, that the U.S. National Debt represents nothing less than a devastating threat to the hopes, dreams, liberty, and freedom of America's presently living children, grandchildren, and the not yet born.

And, in answer to where do America's so-called adults in the room stand regarding the ever-growing threats posed by our country's National Debt and Unfunded Liabilities, most of us seem to fall into one of the following groups:

1. Those who just "tune out" the subjects altogether and bury their heads in the sand (or more fittingly put, "up their backside").

2. Those who refuse to accept or believe that our National Debt and Unfunded Liabilities actually exits.

3. Those who accept that our National Debt and Unfunded Liabilities do exist, but "BS" themselves into believing such debts and obligations don't really matter.

4. Those who accept that our National Debt and Unfunded Liabilities do exist, but "BS" themselves into believing that "the government" will somehow "fix things" (ignoring the fact that "the government" of "we the people" is the cause of our nation's debt problem in the first place).

5. Those who accept that our National Debt and Unfunded Liabilities do exist, and that such are a real problem, but are willing to kick the can of responsibility down the road for future generations of Americans to deal with. And with same attitude are able to look America's young children and grandchildren in the eye, and sleep well at night.

6. Those who view our nation's National Debt and Unfunded Liabilities in rational and level-headed manner, and understand that unsustainable debts of such magnitude will one day result in disastrous economic consequences of unimaginable nature and extent. And with such view strive to make sensible personal preparations for such outcome.

7. Those who view our nation's National Debt and Unfunded Liabilities in rational and level-headed manner, and understand that unsustainable debts of such magnitude will

one day result in disastrous economic consequences of unimaginable nature and extent. And with such view, not only strive to make sensible personal preparations for such outcome. But, also through the power of their vote and other means available to them, unrelentingly demand systematic elimination of the threats posed by our National Debt and Unfunded Liabilities. Through responsible government tax and spend legislation, policies, procedures, budgeting, and as-needed national sacrifice.

And so, the crucial question remains—where do you and I stand?

In the end, our respective answers of course will determine whether we—the now so-called adults in charge—responsibly carry out our citizen-duty. Or, instead, choose to leave our young children and grandchildren of today, and America's generations not yet born, a shameful liberty-threatening legacy of unsustainable debt and unfulfilled promises—and the unthinkable consequences there from.

= = =

"Those who stand for nothing fall for anything."
— Alexander Hamilton (1757-1804)

"You cannot escape the responsibility of tomorrow by evading it today." *— Abraham Lincoln (1809-1865)*

"*The problem is real, and the solution will be painful. We must stabilize and then reduce the national debt, or we could spend $1 trillion a year in interest alone by 2020. There is no easy way out of our debt problem, so everything must be on the table. A sensible, realistic plan requires shared sacrifice – and Washington must lead the way and tighten its belt.*" — *The Moment of Truth: Report of the National Commission on Fiscal Responsibility and Reform, The White House, December 1, 2010*

"*History is littered with examples of major economic and financial crises in countries that have engaged in public spending profligacy. That sad experience should be raising red flags in the United States, where the unsustainable longer-run trajectory of the US public finances is now suggesting the real risk of either a destructive burst of inflation or an outright government debt default. This is particularly the case in today's US context where an ever-increasing portion of the US budget deficit is being financed by foreigners and where entitlement programs threaten over the longer haul to compound an already highly compromised public finance position.*" — *Desmond Lachman, a resident Fellow at the American Enterprise Institute (AEI). Re: On the Fiscal Road to Serfdom, American Enterprise Institute. October 22, 2009*

"*The consequences arising from the continual accumulation of public debts in other countries ought to admonish us to be careful to prevent their growth in our own.*" — *John Adams (1735-1826), a U.S. Founding Father; First U.S. Vice President; Second U.S. President*

Climate Change:
"Another Side of the Story"

"Global climate is always changing in accordance with natural causes and recent changes are not unusual . . ."; "Carbon dioxide and other 'greenhouse gas' emissions from human activity – energy production, transportation, cement production, heating and cooling, etc. – appear to have only a very small impact on global climate . . ." – The International Climate Science Coalition (ICSC), a coalition of 140+ climate scientists, economists, and engineers. As reported in the "Core Principles" section of its website (accessed 02/09/2019).

"We, the undersigned, having assessed the relevant scientific evidence, do not find convincing support for the hypothesis that human emissions of carbon dioxide are causing, or will in the foreseeable future cause, dangerous global warming." – a coalition of 140+ climate scientists, economists, and engineers, from the U.S. and 21 other countries, listed in "The Climate Scientists' Register" of the International Climate Science Coalition (ICSC) [accessed at http://www.climatescienceinternational.org on 02/10/2019].

The Wednesday, November 28, 2018 edition of our local newspaper, the *Parsons Sun,* included a front-page article titled, *"Report: Climate change to impact ag, infrastructure and health of Kansans."* Followed by a more recent February 8, 2019, page 3 article, titled *"Democrats Seek Green New Deal to Address Climate Change."* These being but a couple of the countless pro and con alarmist publications nationwide, that relate to the emotionally-charged money-driven "Climate Change" (formally "Global Warming") movement.

A much hyped movement that the radical political-left continues to embrace in its increasingly socialist aligned platform. One also faithfully supported by a renewable-energy industry feeding off of lucrative taxpayer-funded subsidies.

Yes, as 2019 estimates show, for example, that: opioid overdose deaths in the U.S. will increase from 33,100 in 2015 to 81,700 in 2025 (a 147 percent increase); and shamefully we have some 500,000 homeless military veterans on our streets, and some 22 veterans commit suicide each and every day; and our southern U.S. border continues to be overran with illegal aliens, and drug and human trafficking; and U.S.-hating Iran keeps chanting "death to America"; and our National Debt keeps growing out-of-control; and etc.; etc., . . . The radical political-left keeps pushing an intentionally distracting, unnecessary, and commonsense-futile agenda supposedly aimed at controlling the Earth's ever-changing climate.

And, as the radical-left, and the indisputably politically-biased so-called mainstream news media, continue to ensure that we are smothered with the "pro" climate change propaganda — this Section offers a fitting and appropriate "another side of the story."

Reportedly — the Planet Earth is about 4.5 billion years old; the earliest fossil evidence of modern human existence, along with stone tools, date to about 300,000 years ago; World industrialization started in Western Europe in the late 1700s and early 1800s; the first considered safe and practical oil engine was developed in 1873 (about 146 years ago); in the remote past, Kansas was covered by seas; and people first came to Kansas some 11,000 to 12,000 years ago, during the last of the most recent Ice Ages.

And, although Kansas was not glaciated (covered with glaciers/sheets of ice) at that time, the climate was cooler and less seasonal than today, and huge animals such as mammoth and mastodon roamed the area until a gradual "warming trend" brought an end to our most recent Ice Age, and mass extinctions occurred — "around 10,000 years ago!"

Long, long before we mere humans fired up our gasoline engines, coal-fired furnaces; and other fossil fuel burning, carbon dioxide emitting, technologies. And, long before we started putting concern about our so-called "carbon footprint," and our delusional-craving to control our 4.5 billion year old Planet Earth's ever-changing climate, ahead of other more pressing and truly survival-rooted matters.

Matters such as: the safety of our schools, places of worship, and other areas of public assembly, from murderous atrocities; our nation's ever-spreading addictive drugs epidemic; the safety and security of our nuclear-powered electric plants and electrical power grids; control of nuclear weapons, both foreign and domestic; security of our U.S. borders; U.S.-beneficial immigration policies; and a rapidly growing U.S. National Debt that, for the first time ever, surpassed $22 trillion in 2019; etc.

Human serenity and survival seems to ultimately rely heavily upon our ability and willingness to accept the things we cannot change, courage to change the things we can, and wisdom to know the difference. A perspective likely important to keep in mind, as we try our best to wade through and responsibly deal with the smothering load of past, present, and future agenda-driven information about our Planet Earth's ever-changing climate. A climate that reportedly has, over billions of years, so far included some five "Ice Age" cycles — without the aid of we mere humans.

And, when faced with related warnings, predictions, government-mandates, etc., that don't seem to satisfy the common sense test, it is likely especially important that we identify and critique the source, and also, as they say — "follow the money."

Such as the sources of the long list of spectacularly wrong predictions made around 1970 when the "green holy day" (aka Earth Day) started.

Predictions such as, "It is already too late to avoid mass starvation," as declared by Denis Hayes, the chief organizer for Earth Day, in the Spring **1970** issue of *The Living Wilderness.*

And, the January **1970** *Life* reporting that, "Scientists have solid experimental and theoretical evidence to support the following predictions: In a decade, urban dwellers will have to wear gas masks to survive air pollution...by **1985** air pollution will have reduced the amount of sunlight reaching the earth by one half...."

Or, American biologist Paul R. Ehrlich's most alarmist scenario for the **1970** Earth Day issue of *The Progressive*, assuring readers that between **1980** and **1989**, some 4 billion people, including 65 million Americans, would perish in the "Great Die-Off." The same Paul Ehrlich who is often accredited with the following quotation, *"The fluttering of a butterfly's wings can effect climate changes on the other side of the planet."*

The above being but a few of the onslaught countless dire "Climate Change" agenda driven predictions that continue to this day.

Predictions that refuse to acknowledge that the present day Great Lakes were carved out by glaciers, advancing and retreating over thousands of years of the Earth's dramatic temperature cycling—and long before humankind's so-called carbon footprint from the use of fossil fuels.

Predictions that intentionally fail to stress, for example, that "climate" has been changing since the Earth was formed - some 4.5 billion years ago. Climate changes on every time scale — whether decades, centuries or millennia.

Predictions that conveniently never acknowledge that, for example, the climate of Greenland was warm enough for farming around the year 1100 A.D., but by 1500, the Little Ice Age drove Norse settlers out.

And, predictions that, by design, never include the following fact-based findings from the International Climate Science Coalition (ICSC), a coalition of 140+ climate scientists, economists, and engineers (As reported in the "Core Principles" section of its website [accessed 02/09/2019]):

1. Global climate is always changing in accordance with natural causes and recent changes are not unusual.

2. Science is rapidly evolving away from the view that humanity's emissions of carbon dioxide and other 'greenhouse gases' are a cause of dangerous climate change.

3. Climate models used by the IPCC* fail to reproduce know past climates without manipulation and therefore lack scientific integrity needed for use in climate prediction and related policy decision-making. (* Intergovernmental Panel on Climate Change.)

4. The UN IPCC* and the assertions of IPCC* executives too often seriously miss-represent the conclusions of their own scientific reports. (* United Nations Intergovernmental Panel on Climate Change.)

5. Claims that 'consensus' exists among climate experts regarding the causes of the modest warming of the past century are contradicted by thousands of independent scientists.

6. Carbon dioxide is not a pollutant – it is a necessary reactant in plant photosynthesis and so is essential for life on Earth.

7. Research that identifies the Sun as a major driver of global climate change must be taken more seriously.

8. Global cooling has presented serious problems for human society and the environment throughout history while global warming has generally been highly beneficial.

9. It is not possible to reliably predict how climate will change in the future, beyond the certainty that multi-decadal warming and cooling trends, and abrupt changes, will all continue, underscoring a need for effective adaptation.

10. Since science and observation have failed to substantiate the human-caused climate change hypothesis, it is premature to damage national economies with `carbon' taxes, emissions trading or other schemes to control 'greenhouse gas' emissions.

History attests that it is likely that we will long be saturated with dire "Climate Change" predictions, and other claims that our only hope is the self-serving, control over our lives power of the radical political-left. Depending of course upon them being given unrestricted access to the taxpayer-funded public treasury. By way of votes cast through ignorance or intent.

Therefore, in the struggle to survive the ever-spreading "pandemic of lunacy" gripping much of our world, it is important that one's perspective include this "Another Side of the Climate Change Story.

And, when faced with "Global Warming"/"Climate Change" related warnings, predictions, government-mandates, etc., especially those that don't seem to satisfy the commonsense test, it is especially important that we "identify and critique the source," and also, as they say — "follow the money."

= = =

"Knowledge will forever govern ignorance, and a people who mean to be their own Governors, must arm themselves with the power knowledge gives." *— James Madison (1751-1836), 4 the U.S. President; one of U.S. Founding Fathers.*

"Refusal to believe until proof is given is a rational position; denial of all outside of our own limited experience is absurd." *— Annie Besant (1847-1933), British socialist; author; theosophist, women's rights activist.*

Immigration, Dreams, Socialism, & Safe Spaces

Absolute self-destructive lunacy includes any "failure to grasp" that the United States (or any other sovereign nation) must be able to control people entering it. As is also any failure to support as-required border security and commonsense merit-based immigration policies.

Furthermore, no nation is under any obligation to let any non-citizen or otherwise unauthorized resident enter it, and accepting either is a completely voluntary thing, to be done at the sole discretion of and benefit to the accepting nation.

As with many other countries, the United States has benefitted greatly from various past immigration, and can do so now and in the future under strictly enforced and carefully vetted merit-based acceptance criteria. Policies ensuring a benefit to our nation and not harm to its legal residents and citizens.

The United States is the historically-proven most generous nation on Earth, and has time and again extended a helping hand to people truly in need from other countries. However, to do so under circumstances that are not beneficial to the U.S., or are otherwise harmful to its legal residents and citizens, is clearly suicidal. For example, we (the U.S.) must not allow those to come here who carry disease, who are violent, who wish to undermine our way of life, or in other ways will do our nation harm. Therefore, standards for acceptance are not only essential but indisputably crucial.

Unfortunately, however, presently and for too many years past, the U.S. immigration system has been a nation-destroying disaster. The southern border, lacking a physical security wall, is dangerously porous. And, despite Border Security efforts, is routinely breached by persons pursuing illegal entry.

As others with visas enter legally, but stay beyond the expiration date. Such people by their very existence inside our borders are then truly lawbreakers, some of whom commit other crimes.

The Cost of Illegal Immigration: Various 2019 estimates have reported the monetary cost of illegal aliens to the U.S. taxpayer to be in the area of $100 billion to $338 billion annually. Based on estimates varying widely, and depending upon the source of the numbers and what cost-items are used to comprise the total.

For example, 2017 Federation for American Immigration Reform (FAIR) reporting showed the annual cost to be $155 billion. Whereas, as reported by Judicial Watch, December 2017, a detailed analysis of federal, state, and local programs that include education, medical care, law enforcement, and welfare, the monetary cost of Illegal Immigration is reportedly costing U.S. Taxpayers at least $134.9 Billion a year. While a study by the Center for Immigration Studies has reported the cost to be a much higher $338.3 billion.

Various annual estimates of illegal immigration costs have included, for example: $22 billion for social services; $2.2 billion for food assistance; $2.5 billion for Medicaid, $29 billion for education; $3 million per day to incarcerate illegal immigrants who comprise 30 percent of all federal prison inmates; $90 billion for welfare; $46 billion for deportation; and $200 billion in suppressed American wages.

Furthermore, related reporting has shown, for example, that illegal alien women had 297,000 children in 2014 at a cost of $2.4 billion. And, although illegal immigrants are technically not eligible for welfare services, Medicaid has historically paid for delivery and post-partum care for at least a few months. And, anyway you dice or slice it, the U.S. is currently spending far more annually cover costs of illegal aliens, than

Congress has as of this writing been willing to fund for a security wall on our southern border.

The Cause of Illegal Immigration: Our nation's failed immigration policies are in large measure the result of years and years of using the arms of government to feed the cravings for cheap labor and votes. As "we the people" — through our elected government representatives — have time and again failed to seriously demand otherwise by way of informed and responsible voting.

Regarding Deferred Action for Childhood Arrivals (DACA): "DACA" is the program giving temporary protection to certain individuals illegally arriving in the U.S. as children, reportedly totaling some 800,000 or more, and often distractingly referred to as **"Undocumented"** Immigrants/Migrants and/or "Dreamers." Congress should stop passing-the-buck, and immediately and responsibly deal with this long-standing issue, along with our other immigration control policy-shortfalls as well.

Starting with immediate support of President Trump's list of required immigration control measures. Such as: construction of the proposed security wall on our southern border; application of other border control enhancements; bringing an end to chain migration and the visa lottery system; and implementation of a merit-based immigration policy.

As well as responsible congressional consideration of a pathway to legal residency and ultimate citizenship for appropriate DACA individuals.

In doing so, we should dispense with distracting labels such as **"Undocumented"** Immigrants/Migrants," "Dreamers," etc. Regardless of the sugar-coated agenda-driven labels, persons illegally entering the U.S. are just that—**"illegal"**! And what's with the DACA **"Dreamers"** tag anyhow? Are we to believe that the millions upon millions of children of "**Legal**" U.S. citizens do not also have hopes and dreams? Including the countless thousands now living in cars, on the street, under bridges, or in subsidized shelters, etc.

With respect to immigrants granted legal entry to the U.S.:
If their plans are to learn and speak English, assimilate U.S. culture, respect and defend our U.S. Constitution, and strive to be productive, self-supporting members of our nation— then **welcome**! If not, and they wish to impose otherwise on our nation, then they should immediately leave the U.S. and apply their energies and intentions where they came from or elsewhere.

And to others who are hell-bent to turn the U.S. into an abyss of socialism (a stepping stone to communism): Please leave and set up residence in any of the various failed countries on this earth that continue to disregard the following cautionary quote from Margaret Thatcher: *"The problem with socialism is that you eventually run out of other people's money."*

In closing this Section on Immigration, Dreams, Socialism, & Safe Spaces: This writer is not "offended" by views counter to those expressed herein. Nor, will such drive me to seek refuge in a taxpayer funded "Safe Space" in one of our nation's colleges or universities.

Of serious concern, however, is any failure to recognize the critical importance of protecting and securing our U.S. Constitution, borders, common-language English, and common-culture founded on Judeo-Christian values.

Well-founded concerns that also include the unsettling prospects of one day entrusting the fate of our nation to those who have been educated, pampered, indoctrinated, and accommodated, to close their minds to (and seek refuge from) the free speech of others that they consider uncomfortable, offensive, or threatening. A mindset thankfully absent from our nation's Founding Fathers as they, through yet unmatched wisdom and insight, established our envy of the world Constitutional Republic, and the precious liberty and freedom for which it stands. A mindset thankfully also absent from the countless who have over the many years since, worked, fought, sacrificed, and otherwise strived, to protect, defend, and preserve such.

= = =

"My reading of history convinces me that most bad government results from too much government." – Thomas Jefferson (1743-1826), a U.S. Founding Father; principle author of the Declaration of Independence; 3rd U.S. President.

But Then . . . Along Came "President Trump"!

> *"Together, We will make America strong again. We will make America wealthy again. We will make America proud again. We will make America safe again. And yes, together, we will make America great again. Thank you. God bless you. And God bless America."* — *Donald J. Trump (1946-), 45th U.S. President.*

It was supposed to be a slam-dunk!

Starting with 17 candidates, the Republican Party's brutal and self-devouring primary had ended with one sole survivor, Donald Trump. The Democrat primary, beginning with three candidates, had soon became a race between Hillary Clinton and Bernie Sanders. With Sanders ultimately endorsing Clinton, as hacked e-mails exposed that top DNC officials had early-on dismissed Sanders as a viable candidate and attempted to undermine and derail his campaign.

Yes, the 2016 presidential election was supposed to have been a done deal! Millions had been given and promised a seemingly endless list of "free-stuff" from our trillions of dollars in-debt public treasury. As a shameful many others had been promised positions of power and influence throughout a long-bloated Federal Government bureaucracy.

Furthermore, years upon years of effort had been invested in promoting victimhood, racial/social unrest, and an array of other divide-and-conquer agendas. Political-correctness had been widely entrenched as weapons against truth, fact, reality, free speech, and common sense. In turn, the so-called mainstream media and entertainment-industry elite had faithfully saturated the country with politically biased venom. And, a "Deep State" (liberty-threatening manipulators within the IRS, FBI, and other government agencies) was firmly and confidently established, entrenched, and committed to disrupt and roadblock any serious threat to the "status-quo."

Yes, our U.S. borders would soon continue to be essentially open to all, providing a growing "voter-base" for some, and endless source of "cheap labor" for others. And, essentially forever secure would be the positions of power, influence, and corruption within the self-sustaining partnership between the radical/irresponsible elements of both the political-left and political-right—the entrenched base of irresponsible career politicians, lobbyists, and bureaucrats—the Washington DC "Swamp."

But then . . . along came "President Trump"! A wealthy businessman; Washington "outsider" — a threat to the "swamp." A president putting U.S. interests above that of other nations, and U.S. citizens' rights above the welfare of illegal aliens; striving to replace nation-destructive political correctness with truth, fact, reality, and common sense; publicly declaring radical/Islamic terrorists to be "radical/Islamic terrorists"; committed to the seemingly impossible task of "Making America Great Again"; donating his taxpayer-funded salary to charity; and expressing a Merry Christmas Wish as a "Merry Christmas" Wish!

A U.S. President who, during his first year in office, racked up more America-preserving accomplishments than most if not all his predecessors! Including an array of thought by many to be impossible endeavors, such as: "The biggest Tax Cut and Reform Bill in America's history"; "Destruction of the ISIS caliphate"; "Historically unmatched booster-shot to U.S. economy"; "3.7 Million New Jobs"; "3.5 Million People Lifted Off Food Stamps"; "400,00 New Manufacturing Jobs"; and "The Lowest Unemployment Rate in Half a Century"!

These being but a few of hundreds of crucial achievements by a President Trump administration that, as of this writing, continues to walk-the-talk on "Making America Great Again"! All while swimming upstream against opposition in both political parties; a hostile mainstream news media; an on-going, nation-damaging hissy-fit from election sore-losers; and a "deep state" committed to our President's failure — even if harmful to our country and threatening to our liberty.

And despite the shameful, unrelenting, nation-destructive anti-Trump behavior of the radical-left, President Trump will likely be one of the, if not the, most liberty-saving and otherwise nation-beneficial U.S. Presidents in our country's history. For certain, had the "Deep State's" pick, Hilary Clinton been elected, the U.S. as we have long known it would by now have been over. And rapidly sliding into the liberty-destroying economic-disaster of fascism and socialism—the stepping stones to communism.

But what does this writer know . . . for I am just one among the deplorables defeated Hillary Clinton once referred to. And, by way of this book just possibly may offend someone, and as a result, be labeled by the unrelenting, reality-denying, politically-correct as racist, sexist, homophobic, xenophobic, and Islamaphobic, and/or an array of countless other "-ists" and "-phobics."

=   =   =

"So to all Americans, in every city near and far, small and large, from mountain to mountain, and from ocean to ocean, hear these words: You will never be ignored again. Your voice, your hopes, and your dreams will define our American destiny. And your courage and goodness and love will forever guide us along the way."
— Donald J. Trump (1946-), 45th U.S. President.

"As long as you're going to be thinking anyway, think big."
— Donald J. Trump (1946-), 45th U.S. President.

Violating
The Public Trust

On Tuesday, January 15, 2019, a federal judge in New York blocked the Trump administration from asking about U.S. citizenship in the upcoming 2020 Census, reportedly finding that to do so would "violate the public trust." As a considerable number of U.S. taxpayers (the ultimately accountable for government spending) feel it irresponsible not to keep tabs on such commonsense information.

And, speaking of "the public trust" — somewhere on our gift-of-life journey, many if not most of us sooner or later grasp that "nothing is truly free." Nevertheless, this inescapable reality is often ignored, especially as we partake of the array of so-called "freebies" offered by the Facebooks, Googles, and other Internet-based companies, etc.

For example, such companies obviously spend untold billions of dollars to collect, store, and otherwise process billions upon billions of text/audio/photo/etc. files (data), and to make a selective amount of such available to millions of people worldwide. Including people like me who have to date not purchased a single item as the result of their advertising, nor have knowingly paid them a cent otherwise.

However, for the privilege of using their so-called "freebies," I and millions of others knowingly or unknowingly provide the Facebooks, Googles, etc., with access to a magnitude of our "personal information." Such as, our contacts list; phone/text/photo files; Internet search history; political leanings; purchase history; age; gender; marital status; address; etc., etc., etc. And, as a result, such companies likely know much more about us than our federal government does. That is, unless our government is among those who pay or "hack" the Facebooks, Googles, etc., for the massive "data" they collect and store (in essence forever).

And, it doesn't defy logic to consider that the collection, storage, and otherwise commercial use of such massive amounts of data (including our personal information), represents a potential threat to the public trust that far outweighs the aforementioned New York federal judge's concerns, i.e., his worry about a U.S. Constitution-permitted census attempting to determine how many U.S. citizens, and non-citizens, reside within our country's borders. Questions that the Facebooks, Googles, etc., likely already have the answers to.

All of which seems to make it more and more crucial that—whether our personal information is collected commercially or by our government—"we the people" always be responsibly mindful of the historical insight and wisdom emphasized by the below indisputably apt quotations.

= = =

"The control of information is something the elite always does, particularly in a despotic form of government. Information, knowledge, is power. If you can control information, you can control people." — *Tom Clancy (1947-2013), American novelist.*

"Democracy must be built through open societies that share information. When there is information, there is enlightenment. When there is debate, there are solutions. When there is no sharing of power, no rule of law, no accountability, there is abuse, corruption, subjugation and indignation." — *Atifete Jahjaga (1975-), 3rd President of Kosovo; First female President of the Republic of Kosovo.*

"Knowledge will forever govern ignorance, and a people who mean to be their own Governors, must arm themselves with the power knowledge gives." — *James Madison (1751-1836), 4th U.S. President; one of U.S. Founding Fathers.*

"At his best, man is the noblest of all animals; separated from law and justice he is the worst." — Aristotle (384-322 BC), ancient Greek philosopher; scientist; along with Plato, considered the "Father of Western Philosophy."

"A politics of vengeance is not politics. Revenge is a recklessness towards the future in a vain attempt to make the present abolish a suffering which is already past." — Bernard Crick (1929-2008), British political theorist; democratic socialist.

"A Bill of Rights is what the people are entitled to against every government, and what no just government should refuse, or rest on inference." — Thomas Jefferson (1743-1826), 3rd U.S. President: one of U.S. Founding Fathers.

"The Framers of the Bill of Rights did not purport to "create" rights. Rather, they designed the Bill of Rights to prohibit our Government from infringing rights and liberties presumed to be preexisting." — William J. Brennan, Jr. (1906-1997), Associate Justice of U.S. Supreme Court from 1956-1990.

Radical-Militant Islam

"Ancient-rooted evils waging World War III against twenty-first century civilization"

> *"The parallels between 9/11 and Pearl Harbor are striking. In each instance there were warning signs before the attack, and in each instance our government failed to connect the dots."* — Diane Watson (1933-), U.S. Representative, 2003-2011.
>
> *"History is a vast early warning system."* — Norman Cousins (1915-1990), American political journalist; author; professor.

Just like now happening in England, Germany, and elsewhere in the World, we U.S. citizens can lose our country without, so-to-speak, a shot being fired. Simply by tolerating open borders; not maintaining an immigration policy based on merit; accepting immigrants who refuse to assimilate our U.S. common-language English and common-culture founded on Judeo-Christian values; and not exercising responsible voting in our nation's elections.

While, at the same time, self-destructively ignoring the ongoing existence of the ancient-rooted threat of radical-militant Islam and Sharia-law. A sinister and savagely cruel threat to life and liberty that continues to wage war against 21st century civilization — with the U.S. as a primary target.

A critical question and deep concern rests, therefore, in the "true intentions" of the various Muslim individuals that are already seated, or about to be seated, in a number of U.S. political offices, as well as others seeking such positions of political power and influence. That is, do they "truly" hold allegiance to our U.S. Constitution . . . or do they openly or covertly hold allegiance to Sharia-law and/or other radical-militant Islam teachings, etc.?

On Thursday, January 03, 2019, during swearing-in ceremonies of members of the new 116th U.S. Congress, Rashida Tlaib (D-Michigan) and Ilhan Omar (D-Minnesota), the first two Muslim women to be elected to the U.S. Congress, chose to take their oaths of office — not on the Christian Bible — but on the Quran, Islam's holiest text.

The Quran made its first appearance in the U.S. Congress swearing-in ceremonies in 2007, when Keith Ellison of Minnesota became the first-ever Muslim member of Congress and chose to use the Quran to take his oath. While the Bible is by far the most common object used in swearing-in ceremonies, the U.S. Constitution includes no requirement that the Christian text — or any other text or object — be used.

And although **Article VI, Clause 3** of the Constitution requires that senators and representatives "be bound by Oath or Affirmation" to support the Constitution, the same clause ends with the declaration that "no religious Test shall ever be required as a Qualification to any Office or public Trust under the United States."

As applies to all taking same oath—"time" and "individual behavior" will reveal the ultimate sincerity of all persons making a sworn commitment to *"support and defend the Constitution of the United States against all enemies, foreign and domestic."*

In the meantime, it is to America's peril that we fail to understand and guard against the fact that our "liberty and freedom ensuring" United States Constitution, and "liberty and freedom destroying" Islamic Sharia-Law, cannot co-exist!

In speeches, September 29, 2014, to the United Nations General Assembly, and six months later, on March 03, 2015, before a special joint-meeting of our U.S. Congress, Israeli Prime Minister Netanyahu delivered very strong, rational, and plain-spoken warnings.

Indisputably justified warnings about the growing threat of radical/militant Islam, and why ISIS must be defeated and Iran must never be allowed to gain nuclear weapons capability.

In his September 29, 2014 speech he strongly cautioned: *"It's not militants. It's not Islam. It's militant Islam. Typically, its first victims are other Muslims, but it spares no one. Christians, Jews, Yazidis, Kurds – no creed, no faith, and no ethnic group is beyond its sights. And it's rapidly spreading in every part of the world. You know the famous American saying: "All politics is local"? For the militant Islamists, "All politics is **global**." Because their ultimate goal is to dominate the world."*

Clearly, therefore—not only America—but all civilized societies worldwide must guard against the ancient-rooted threat of radical-militant Islam. By, as a minimum: securing one's country's borders; voting responsibly; enforcing a carefully vetted merit-based immigration policy; enforcing assimilation of the common-language and common-culture of one's country; and, conducting close oversight of all aspects of educational systems, regarding who is teaching the nation's children and what are they being taught.

At stake, nothing less than the too often taken for granted liberty and freedom of those now fortunate to experience such, and the hopes and dreams of the countless oppressed now seeking that which they are denied.

Hopefully, the herein warnings about radical-militant Islam, and related atrocities in the U.S. homeland and elsewhere around the World, are sufficient wake-up calls. If not, a wide selection of fact-based readings are available about this looming menace that should awaken even the most complacent or terminally-in-denial among us.

Such as, "Because They Hate," by Brigitte Gabriel; and "Killing Life, Liberty, & Pursuit of Happiness," by this writer; and an array of other fact-based sources.

However, "where" one gains factual-enlightenment is not what matters. Indisputably crucial, however, is one's dedication to seeking truth, recognizing and accepting reality, and responsibly applying the knowledge and wisdom gained therefrom!

= = =

"We are at war, and our security as a nation depends on winning that war." – Condoleezza Rice (1954-), National Security Advisor during first term of U.S. President George W. Bush; 66th U.S. Secretary of State; first female African-American Secretary of State.

"Terrorism is not an expression of rage. Terrorism is a political weapon. Remove a government's façade of infallibility, and you remove its people's faith." – Daniel "Dan" Brown (1964-)

"We have an American culture and we have an American constitution and anybody who's going to occupy our White House should be living in a pattern that is consistent with our constitution and our culture." – Ben Carson (1951-), Retired Neurosurgeon; Republican presidential candidate, 2015-16.

"We must always take sides. Neutrality helps the oppressor, never the victim. Silence encourages the tormentor, never the tormented." — Eliezer Wiesel (1928-2016), Romanian-born American Jewish writer, professor, political activist, Nobel Laureate, Holocaust survivor.

"Of course, the overwhelming majority of Muslims are not terrorists or sympathetic to terrorists. Equating all Muslims with terrorism is stupid and wrong. But acknowledging that there is a link between Islam and terror is appropriate and necessary." — Ayaan Hirsi Ali (1969-), Somali-born Dutch-American activist; feminist; author.

"Jihad can mean holy war to extremists, but it means struggle to the average Muslim." — Feisal Abdul Rauf (1948-), Egyptian American Sufi Imam; author; activist.

"The purpose of terrorism lies not just in the violent act itself. It is in producing terror. It sets out to inflame, to divide, to produce consequences which they then use to justify further terror." — Tony Blair (1953-), Prime Minister of the United Kingdom, 1997-2007.

"There may be times when we are powerless to prevent injustice, but there must never be a time when we fail to protest." — Eliezer Wiesel (1928-2016), Romanian-born American Jewish writer; professor.

"In the End, we will remember not the words of our enemies, but the silence of our friends." — Martin Luther King, Jr. (1929-1968), American Baptist minister; 1964 Nobel Peace Prize Recipient; First President of Southern Christian Leadership Conference; activist; most visible spokesperson and leader in civil rights movement from 1954 until his assassination in 1968.

Female Genital Mutilation / Cutting (FGM/C)

"To me, it is not racist to demand, 'I will not accept little girls in my country to be forced into marriage, or their genitals to be cut, for them to be pulled out of school, for them to be condemned to a life of submission or violence or death through an honor killing.' What you want for that girl is what you want for your own little girl."
— Ayaan Hirsi Ali (1969-), Politician; Author; Founder of the AHA Foundation, a nonprofit organization for the defense of women's rights. AHA Foundation goal: combat crimes against women and girls such as, child marriage, forced marriages, female genital mutilation, and honor killings.

At the slightest hint of "racism" or "discrimination" or "non-inclusiveness" or "uncaringness"; etc., the so-called mainstream news media and radical-liberal talk-show circus, will rise up in outrage!

And, regardless of whether such claim is real, imagined, mistaken, contrived, or just outright non-existent, these pompous elements of our society will often unrelentingly overwhelm us with 24/7 politically-biased and ratings-lusted propaganda. Until someone has been, as a minimum, branded as an unforgivably despicable social outcast! However, the same self-declared "epitomes of caring" continue to selectively ignore some of our World's undeniably real and ongoing tragedies.

Such as, the millions of past and present women and girls Worldwide who are shamefully subjected to "female genital mutilation/cutting (FGM/C)." More specifically, subjected to the horrific and ancient-rooted practice of piercing, cutting, removing, or sewing closed all or part of a woman's or girl's external genitals for no medical reason. A truly barbaric practice that researchers estimate more than 500,000 girls and women in the United States have experienced or are at risk of being subjected to.

And "why" the continued avoidance of this longstanding and continuing tragedy? Because FGM/C doesn't fit the liberty/nation-destructive narrative!

Yes, FGM/C doesn't serve those who are otherwise preoccupied with more lucrative vote-seeking and/or ratings-craving endeavors. Such as, spinning their agenda-driven pretense about their deep concern for humankind.

Especially, for example, regarding the welfare of illegal aliens and the children used to aid their self-serving illegal invasion of our country. For the sake of "votes" and "cheap labor."

According to Public Health Reports / March-April 2016/ Volume 131: In 1996, the U.S. Congress passed legislation making female genital mutilation/cutting (FGM/C) illegal in the United States. Nonetheless, Center of Disease Control (CDC) estimates revealed approximately **513,000** women and girls in the U.S. were at risk for FGM/C or its consequences in YR 2012, which was **more than three times** higher than earlier estimates based on 1990 data. And, the increase in the number of women and girls younger than 18 years of age at risk for FGM/C was **more than four times** that of previous estimates. The CDC conclusion being, this estimated increase was wholly a result of the **rapid growth in the number of immigrants** from FGM/C practicing countries living in the United States and not from increases in FGM/C prevalence in those countries.

On July 20, 2016, the U.S. Department of Health and Human Services Office on Women's Health (OWH), announced more than $6 million in grant awards over a 3-year period to cities across the nation. Eight sites covering thirteen cities were selected to address the gaps and problems in FGM/C related health care services for women and girls living in the U.S. who experienced FGM/C. The funds were to be used to prevent FGM/C of women and girls living in the U.S. who are at risk for having the procedure conducted here or in another country.

Yes, in excess of a half-million women and young girls now in the United States are at risk of being subjected to FGM/C within our U.S. borders, or temporally taken abroad for this hideous procedure! A shameful practice brought to U.S. soil as the result of immigration to the U.S. from African and Middle Eastern countries and elsewhere. From societies where FGM/C is entrenched in barbaric cultural tradition.

Brought to U.S. soil by individuals having no plans, or U.S.-enforced incentive, to discontinue this truly cruel and most-inhumane procedure, and otherwise "assimilate" U.S. culture and abide by U.S. constitutional law. As the yet untouched among us, through innocent-ignorance or intent, turn our so-called civilized heads away, in favor of countless less-challenging and more self-absorbed causes and distractions. While, in this the 21st century, millions of women and young girls Worldwide continue to suffer deathblows to life, liberty, and pursuit of happiness, at the unspeakably-cruel hand of ancient-rooted FGM/C.

= = =

"There is such a culture of silence about Female Genital Mutilation (FGM/C). If you stand up and say 'This happened to me', people will scrutinize you, but someone has to stand up and say, this can't go on happening. This is a human rights abuse and it has to stop. Until the education of a girl is a right and not a privilege, we are failing our women." — Jaha Dukureh (1989 or 1990-), a Gambian women's right activist; anti-female genital mutilation campaigner. Founder and executive director of Safe Hands for Girls, an organization working to end FGM/C. Dukureh was subjected to female genital mutilation when she was a little more than a week old.

Reckless Absurdities

"The nuclear arms race is like two sworn enemies standing waist deep in gasoline, one with three matches, the other with five." — Carl Sagan (1934-1996), American astronomer; cosmologist.

"The people heard it, and approved the doctrine, and immediately practiced the contrary." — Benjamin Franklin (1706-1705), one of U.S. Founding Fathers; American polymath; author; scientist.

Our country's many responsible inhabitants, striving to do the right thing, are in uphill struggle with a growing mix of daunting obstacles. Including, none the least, an array of "reckless absurdities." What follows are but a randomly-listed few:

(1.) <u>Refusing to accept that "nothing is truly free — someone must pay"</u>: U.S. citizens (and illegal aliens) who continue to demand [and politicians who continue to promise] free healthcare, free food, free housing, free transportation, free education, free smartphones, etc., — while facing a rapidly growing national debt that, by the arrival of 2019, exceeded $22 trillion (over $67,000 per citizen; $179,000 thousand per taxpayer). A staggering obligation that does not include our in excess of $122 trillion of Unfunded Liabilities (over $1,000,000 per taxpayer) — consisting of Medicare Parts A, B, and D; Federal Debt held by the Public; plus Federal Employees' & Veterans' Benefits). All in irresponsible defiance of the simple reality that nothing is truly free; someone must eventually pay.

(2.) Blatant public disrespect for "national pride" and "true sacrifice": NFL players and like-behaving others who equate their relatively privileged life circumstances to that of men, women, and children, of the distant past and present, who actually suffered or are suffering the ravages of slavery and other persecution. As said players are paid millions of dollars to "play" on artificial turf, wearing high-tech protective gear, with access to the best health care money can buy. While in turn experiencing security and freedom created, protected, and preserved through the sacrifice of countless others.

(3.) Refusal to accept that the only money "the government" has is "our money" and/or "our debt": "We the people" continuing to tolerate, encourage, and often demand, unrestricted, self-destructive, government spending. While ignoring or ignorant of the reality that the only money "the government" has is that which it taxes from us, or borrows from us and other countries, or prints. With money borrowed becoming our debt, additionally printed money ultimately devaluing our U.S. currency, and taxes increasingly reducing our net (left available for our use) income.

(4.) <u>Self-destructive Denial or Ignorance of World history</u>: Persons who have, for example, nation-destructively equated U.S. President Trump and/or his predecessors, with past and present barbaric dictators, such as Germany's Adolf Hitler, Russia's/Soviet Union's Joseph Stalin, and North Korea's Kim Jong-un, etc. While in doing so demonstrating their blatant disregard and/or dangerous ignorance of world history, as it truly relates to the life/liberty/freedom destroying atrocities of the Nazi Party, Communist Party, Marxism, Leninism, Fascism, etc.

(5.) <u>Raising our nation's young to be frightened by and unable to cope with the spoken word</u>: Teaching our youth to, in the face of what they view as "offensive speech," cuddle up with a cup of hot chocolate, a stress-relieving pet-puppy/kitten, and staff of counsellors, in one of our growing numbers of taxpayer-funded "Safe Spaces" being established in our nation's colleges and universities. As others at great (often ultimate) sacrifice are called upon to protect the freedom of even those who choose to abuse it.

= = =

Hopefully, those we depend upon to protect our liberty do not one day choose to "take a knee" or "scramble for a Safe Space," and leave our precious, envy of the world, constitutional republic, at the mercy of the consequences of these and other examples of "reckless absurdity." And, as a result, putting at risk the inalienable (God-given) rights to life, liberty, and pursuit of happiness of present and future generations of Americans.

"At what point will Washington throw in the towel and stop mortgaging the future of our children and grandchildren -- when interest on national debt exceeds total annual revenues or when lending countries lose confidence in our ability to repay our debt?" – Edward Inghrim (1943-2017). [Words from "The national debt is even worse than you think", Lehigh Valley Live, March 20, 2017]

"Back in 2008, candidate Obama called a $10 trillion national debt 'unpatriotic' - serious talk from what looked to be a serious reformer. Yet by his own decisions, President Obama has added more debt than any other president before him, and more than all the troubled governments of Europe combined. One president, one term, $5 trillion in new debt." – Paul Ryan (1970-), 54th Speaker of the U.S. House of Representatives since 2015.

"For 50 years, nuclear power stations have provided three products which only a lunatic could want: bomb-explosive plutonium, lethal radioactive waste and electricity so dear it has to be heavily subsidized. They leave to future generations the task, and most of the cost, of making safe sites that have been polluted half-way to eternity." – James Buchan (1954-), Scottish novelist; historian.

Gun Control

> *"It's not a gun control problem; it's a cultural control problem."*
> — Bob Barr (1948-); Georgia U.S. Congressman, 1995-2003.
>
> *"In 1939, Germany established gun control. From 1939 to 1945, six million Jews and seven million others unable to defend themselves were exterminate."* — Joe Wurzelbacher (1973-); American conservative activist; commentator; correspondent.

If one were to rank examples of lunacy, disarming law-abiding citizens would have to rank extremely high on the list. For, evil seeking to do harm to innocent others could care less about laws, rules, regulations, or "signs" forbidding their heinous acts. Or about other "feel good barriers" to their choice of weapons, etc.

For example, it was not a troubled teenager with a so-call "assault-rifle," but rather two adult men, ages 27 and 40, using not a gun, but rather a fertilizer-based bomb, who killed 168 people, injured more than 680 others, destroyed or damaged some 325 buildings, causing damage estimated to be $652 million—in downtown Oklahoma City, Oklahoma on April 19, 1995.

Likewise, on November 5, 2009, it was not a teen with an abusive home/social life, but rather a 39 year old U.S. Army psychiatrist and Medical Corps Major who—after shouting "Aliahu Akbar!"—killed 13 people and wounded at least 30 others, in a "mass murder" he carried out at the Fort Hood Military Base, Texas, using not an "assault rifle"—but rather, a "pistol." A tragedy that would have been much worse, had the murderer not eventually been felled by a civilian police sergeant armed with a "gun." A senseless tragedy that could have been much less severe, had the murder not had benefit of a "gun free zone" to carry out this barbaric atrocity---yes, you read that right, "a gun free zone" on a U.S. Military Base!

The above are of course just a couple of unsettling reminders that evil can be embodied in a wide range of beings—with access to essentially a boundless nature of weapons. Evidencing the importance that we unrelentingly hold our government accountable for effectively carrying out its U.S. Constitution granted powers and responsibilities for protection of U.S. citizens. While never infringing upon the Second Amendment rights of law-abiding citizens.

= = =

"Make no mistake about it. Gun control is not about crook control. It's about America control." – Derrick Grayson, Minister; Network Engineer; ran for Georgia's U.S. Senate seat in 2014 and 2016.

A "Less Than" Warm-Hearted Message to Radical-Left

> *"We all learned in kindergarten that the beginning is a very good place to start. As we have this debate on illegal immigration and illegal entry into this country, let's begin at the very beginning by sealing the borders to this great nation." — Marsha Blackburn (1952-), American politician; U.S. Senator from Tennessee.*

This book or other writings about lunacy would be grossly amiss, if failing to highlight the nation-destructive behavior of the radical-left under the guise of their "unique concern and caring" about others.

Hence, the basis for the following open message which is upfront acknowledged to be a bit "less than" warm-hearted:

To: Where the Shoe Fits . . . "Your pompous and otherwise grandiose outcries; your disruptive public demonstrations; and your 24/7 biased-media support,—being carried out in defiance of our r U.S. Constitution, U.S. Flag, U.S. National Anthem, control of U.S. borders, support of our common U.S. language-English, and common U.S. culture founded on Judeo-Christian values,--of course have absolutely nothing to do with your self-proclaimed "unique concern or caring" for fellow human beings. Other than possibly in the minds of a relative few very misguided and innocently ignorant souls caught up in this among your latest attempts to deny, discredit, and disrupt the nation-saving efforts of the Trump administration.

No, your above referenced radical political-left agenda driven behaviors are not about concern and caring for illegal aliens and/or the children they (not the U.S.) put at risk. Rather, such behaviors have everything to do with "votes"; "cheap labor"; and other matters concerning "money." That is, votes for the democrat party; cheap labor for certain business interests irrespective of political affiliation; and money from the public treasury to pay the ever-growing tab for accommodating those choosing to disrespect our borders and abuse our nation's generosity. Money that represents an "expense" to the public treasury (taxpayer) and "income/profit" to the array of businesses and so-called charitable organizations that feed off of legal/illegal immigration traffic.

Furthermore, if you truly have the craving to demonstrate your self-proclaimed "concern and caring" for others, you really need not rely upon illegal aliens entering through our Southern borders or elsewhere. You need only to open your eyes and hearts to "our" nation's long suffering citizens.

For example, it has been estimated that within our U.S. borders there are already more than a half-million "homeless" human beings. Persons-in-need who are living under bridges, in the streets, etc., and fearfully in doubt where their next meal, shelter, or life-threatening circumstance, etc., will come from. It has also been estimated that about one-fourth of these more than half-million "homeless" are "children." And, it has furthermore been estimated that at least 50,000 of our nation's homeless are "U.S. Veterans."

Most shameful national disasters—right under our noses— that have for years been and still remain unaddressed. An ever-growing tragedy that has yet to draw meaningful attention from the more fortunate and influential among us. Least of all, constructive attention from you the radical political-left, your biased news media, and likeminded others, who are hell-bent to put illegal aliens and criminal aliens above the interests of U.S. citizens. As you continue your centuries-old efforts to destroy our nation with socialist/communist (someone else pays) agendas.

So, here's a truly novel idea, along with a most sincere request directed at you and whomever else the shoe fits (so to speak):

Instead of hanging around here in ceaseless pursuit of way of destroying our constitutional republic and liberty therefrom, and to be ever-plagued by the likes of me and other despicable deplorables that endlessly offend you and get in the way of everything you consider yourself "deserving of" . . . . . . PLEASE "very timely" pack up your things and make a not-round-trip move elsewhere to your socialist/communist dictator-governed country of choice.

In doing so, it is suggested that you give priority consideration to a residence in socialist-destroyed Venezuela or communist/dictator-ravaged North Korea. Where you can best use your own resources and self-proclaimed expertise to — directly on site — demonstrate your "governing skills" and your abundance of "concern and caring" for all those who are struggling to escape to the U.S. or elsewhere.

And for the U.S.-haters, never-Trumpers, and likeminded others, who choose to remain here and continue your disregard for the rights and needs of U.S. citizens, please share your gated communities, personal residences, private clubs, armed security services, and your other personal resources, with the illegal aliens and families thereof that you succeed in adding to the burden of our already much in debt nation.

Thereby taking a special opportunity to publicly evidence the personal embodiment of the unique nature of "concern and caring" the radical political left continues to attribute solely to itself." - - - Signed, *William James Moore* (on behalf of myself and millions of like-minded others).

Abuse of Power

> "**Liberty** may be endangered by the **abuse of liberty**, but also by the **abuse of power**." — James Madison (1751-1836), 4th U.S. President and a U.S. Founding Father.

History supports that "abuse of power" is an age-old human condition. With people, animals and other life forms, the environment, etc., being among the many victims. Casualties of an array of abuses (e.g., physical, psychological, sexual, economic, human rights, etc.). Carried out at times by perpetrators in virtually every aspect of human society (e.g., families; government; news media; social media; religious institutions; educational institutions; law enforcement; medical practice/institutions; financial and charitable institutions; sports and entertainment; business; labor; criminal elements; terrorists, etc.).

History also shows that timely reporting and lawfully-just handling of "abuses of power" are much too often seriously impeded by further — "abuses of power." A truly sad reality that may be undergoing long awaited change, as evidenced by the dramatic increase in public accusations of sexual-related abuses in government, business, sports, entertainment, etc., that seem to take root in the 2018 time frame. Captivating (at least for the moment) a likewise dramatic increase in news reporting and national attention. Time will tell if this notable trend signals and ultimately renders a long past due, lawfully-just, and otherwise constructive outcome.

As will time also reveal the consequences of our willingness or unwillingness to:

(1.) Demand immediate discontinuance and public accounting of the recently revealed special fund, from which over 17 million U.S. taxpayer dollars have reportedly been paid out in some 268 sexual-harassment and other discrimination settlements within the federal government over the past 20 years;

(2.) Demand immediate repeal of the Freedom of Information Act "exemption" that our "servants of the people" have reportedly put in place to preclude public disclosure of pertinent information about above referenced taxpayer-funded settlements. Accompanied by immediate (prior to YR 2018 elections) public accounting regarding who received how much, when, and as the result of the accused/actual abuse of power by whom?);

(3.) Apply and support nation-wide respect for the rights of both the accuser and the accused, including "presumption of innocence" until lawfully proven otherwise. Lest the rights and protection of our U.S. Constitution be disregarded and replaced by mob-rule driven by the absence of clear distinction between an accusation and a lawfully-proven truth.

In our quest to protect ourselves from the abuses of government, we should take special note of the historically-proven wisdom of the below quote of James Madison (1751-1836), 4th U.S. President and a U.S. Founding Father:

"Knowledge will forever govern ignorance, and a people who mean to be their own Governors, must arm themselves with the power knowledge gives."

A quote that has purposefully been repeated within this writing. In this the "information age," where we have more and more information available 24/7 at our fingertips. Overwhelmed with information requiring special due diligence on our part to sort fact from opinion, truth from falsehood, and helpful clarification from harmful distortion. While always cautiously discriminating between responsible "exercise of rightful authority" and blatant "abuse of power."

= = =

"Nearly all men can stand adversity, but if you want to test a man's character, give him power." — *Abraham Lincoln (1809-1865), 16th U.S. President.*

"Can any of you seriously say the Bill of Rights could get through Congress today? It wouldn't even get out of committee."
— F. Lee Bailey (1933-), American former criminal defense attorney.

"In general, the art of government consists of taking as much money as possible from one party of the citizens to give to the other."
— Voltaire (1694-1778), a French Enlightenment writer; historian; philosopher.

"A government which robs Peter to pay Paul can always depend on the support of Paul." — George Bernard Shaw (1856-1950), Irish playwright; critic; polemicist; political activist.

"We don't have a trillion-dollar debt because we haven't taxed enough; we have a trillion-dollar debt because we spend too much."
— Ronald Reagan (1911-2004), 40th U.S. President.

"An Open-Letter" to U.S. Congress

> *"Whenever any form of government becomes destructive of these ends [life, liberty, and the pursuit of happiness] it is the right of the people to alter or abolish it, and to institute new government."*
> — *Thomas Jefferson (1743-1826), 3rd U.S. President.*

To: All members of the U.S. Senate and House of Representatives

Subject: "Violations of the Public Trust"

While the numbers from an array of surveys often vary, the bottom-line indicates a growing public distrust and disapproval of both our U.S. Congress and the news media in general. "Even more alarming":

(1.) Both the congress and news media continue to demonstrate a lack of willingness, competency, and wisdom to correct their shameful violations of the public trust;

(2.) A truly worrisome number of survey respondents reportedly hold the view that both the congress and news media are doing OK;

(3.) It is of course votes (not the tooth fairy) that fill the seats of congress — and enable the incompetent to remain there again and again. And, it is not the tooth fairy who continues to purchase the newspapers and select the TV and other media broadcasts, regardless of distrustful content.

The criticisms included and referenced herein, are of course not aimed at the members of congress and the news media who unrelentingly strive to do what is right for our country.

Much to the contrary, the herein expressed criticisms are directed at those who in any manner constitute, support, and enable our country's foreign and domestic enemies.

Those with aims to, through ignorance or intent, destroy the very "foundation blocks" of our Constitutional Republic — (i.e., our U.S. Constitution; borders, common-language English; and common-culture founded on Judeo-Christian values).

A destruction of long and ongoing status; carried out by a growing number of means. Such as: an out of control and unsustainable national debt; unsecured borders; and lack of a merit-based immigration system.

As well as accommodation of immigrants who refuse to assimilate our country's common-language English and common-culture; attempts to disarm law-abiding citizens; infiltration of our education institutions with those who refuse to teach unbiased, fact-based World and American History, as same institutions and others strive to silence the other-than-radical-liberal free speech of their students and other Americans; etc.

Of course, including this "open-letter" in this self-published book, and posting it on social media, are not done with any delusions that any of those to whom it is aimed will ever see, read, or demonstrate any constructive response to the issues drawn attention to herein.

Concerns that have, over the years, also time and again been elaborated upon in numerous other ways. Such as, through other books; Public Mind articles in local newspapers; postings on social media and on personal web pages/blog sites; as well as via e-mails, formal letters, etc., to various U.S. Presidents and members of Congress.

The same or very similar concerns of those shared and expressed in various ways by millions of other Americans. Serious, reality-based issues expressed by individual Americans who—in the face of an irresponsible government and nation-destructive biased news media, are still driven to do what each we can.   —Sincerely, William James Moore - (on behalf of myself and like-concerned others.)

"I am concerned for the security of our great Nation; not so much because of any threat from without, but because of the insidious forces working from within." — Douglas MacArthur (1880-1964), American five-star general and Field Marshal of the Philippine Army; Chief of Staff of U.S. Army during 1930's; played a prominent role in Pacific theater during World War II.

"It does not require a majority to prevail, but rather an irate, tireless minority keen to set brush fires in people's minds." — Samuel Adams (1722-1803), American statesman; political philosopher; one of U.S. Founding Fathers.

"All that is necessary for the triumph of evil is for good men [and women] to do nothing." — Edmund Burke (1729-1797), Irish statesman; author; orator; political theorist; philosopher.

"Our lives begin to end the day we become silent about things that matter." — Plato (428/427 or 424/423BC – 348/347 BC), Athenian philosopher during Classical period in Ancient Greece; Founder of the Academy, the first institution of higher learning in the Western world.

Choices & Consequences

> *"The Roman Empire was very much like us. They lost their moral core, their sense of values in terms of who they were. And after all of those things converged together, they just went right down the tube very quickly."* — *Ben Carson (1951-), U.S. Secretary of Housing and Urban Development; author and former neurosurgeon.*

As with all countries over time, America has undergone and will continue to be challenged by an array of "cultural changes" — all entailing "choices" and "consequences."

Among our worst choices to date — those resulting in failure to provide our school children and teaching staffs with effective protection from unspeakably horrific massacres.

As should be the case, often there is no shortage of demands for education resources to address needs driven by "advances in technology." However, too often irresponsibly absent are like demands for resources to effectively "protect lives" in our schools against the heinous threats of today's world.

A truly daunting challenge and moral obligation that continues to get side-tracked, buried, and silenced in an abyss of emotions, miss-information; self-serving political agendas, irresponsible news/social media coverage, etc.

A commonsense duty further encumbered by a very unsettling reality. That being, a growing number among us (especially apathetic adults and our more impressionable youth) have even been propagandized with the dangerous delusion that "inanimate objects" (especially guns) somehow have the intent and capability for carrying out murderous or otherwise life threatening acts—"without the hand of humans."

Worse, yet, those offering life-saving, peace-of-mind assuring evidence to the contrary are being shouted-down and demonized as uncaring, irresponsible gun-fanatics, and otherwise socially despicable beings.

Furthermore, crucially important commonsense-rooted information is too often disregarded. For example, not so many years ago (within my and many existing other's lifetimes) guns were much more easily accessible in the U.S. than they are today. And, responsibly supervised shooting clubs, rifle teams, etc., were even accepted on various school premises. Schools that even "back then" also included some students who were, for example: treated unfairly; had an abusive home life; were socially neglected; academically challenged; bullied; and at times, even "offended."

Schools where responsible minded students were not expelled for possession of a simple pocket knife, or for drawing a picture of a weapon or a warrior, or for wearing clothing displaying the U.S. Flag, etc. Schools that (regardless of their students' respective life circumstances) were essentially void of today's murderous atrocities.

So what has changed and why? The answer: Our American "culture"; for a mix of reasons, including the obvious, illusive, and highly controversial.

However, the complexity of the "whys" does not lighten our responsibility for the safety and security of our schools—for the lives of our children and teaching staff. Nor are we absolved from the responsibility to let common sense prevail in our quest for solutions.

Starting with accepting that evil does and will continue to exist. And that persons with murderous aims frankly don't give a damn about laws, policies, age-restrictions, political correctness, "gun-free zone" signs, or offending someone.

Our solutions must provide our schools with at least the same level of protection we demand (and tolerate) when traveling via commercial aircraft, vacationing on luxury cruise ships, and attending professional sports/other entertainment stadiums, etc. And, we must do so "now"—not later. While keeping responsibly in mind that we (and affected others) ultimately reap what we sow.

"On January 21st of 2017, the day after I take the oath of office, Americans will finally wake up in a country where the laws of the United States are enforced. We are going to be considerate and compassionate to everyone. But my greatest compassion will be for our own struggling citizens." — Donald J. Trump (1946-), 45th U.S. President.

"We must reject the idea that every time a law's broken, society is guilty rather than the lawbreaker. It is time to restore the American precept that each individual is accountable for his actions."
        — Ronald Reagan (1911-2004), 40th U.S. President.

"In every single thing you do, you are choosing a direction. Your life is a product of choices." — Dr. Kathleen Hall (1951-), founder and C.E.O of the Stress Institute and the Mindful Living Network.

"I am not arrogant enough to tell you what the future holds, but I am faithful enough to remind you who holds the future." — Steve Maraboli (1975-), motivational speaker; author.

Never Be a Sore Loser!

"You're never a loser until you quit trying." – Mike Ditka (1939-), former American Football player, coach, TV commentator, member of College and Pro Football Halls of Fame.

"The price of success is hard work, dedication to the job at hand, and the determination that whether we win or lose, we have applied the best of ourselves to the task at hand."'
– Vince Lombardi (1913-1970), American football player, coach, executive in National Football League.

As evidenced by so far surviving in spite of myself, over the years many family, friends, and others have been caring enough to share with me an array of voluntary paths to proper behavior and a good life. None the least, the importance of "never being a sore loser" . . . "never resenting the good fortune of others."

Such being a far from trivial bit of important life-guidance that falls in the sack of many crucial others that I still fall terribly short in measuring up to.

For, to this day, I find myself envious, and at times very resentful. For example, of those who "win the various lotteries"!

And, if I had the intelligence-gathering resources of the "deep state"; the reputation-destroying power of the radical-left; and the unrelenting 24/7 support of the biased media, . . . I very likely would harass, shame, and if necessary threaten other winners until they caved in, publically apologized for contaminating the human race with their presence, and swiftly passed their obviously underserved winnings in total to "me" — the truly most deserving.

Never the less, and while burdened with this and many other acknowledged personal flaws and failings, I still find needed comfort and life-sustaining refuge in the realization that I am at least "not" the cause of nor responsible for an array of other despicable things. Such as: hate speech; racial-divide; California's wild fires; floods, hurricanes, tornados; world hunger; gun violence; atrocities carried out by terrorists; police brutality; abuse of illegal aliens; climate change (earlier called "global warming"); inadequate health care; wars and turmoil throughout the World.

As well as: student debt; disease; income inequality; sexual discrimination; white supremacy; divorce; poor gas mileage; highway congestion; the drug addiction crisis; crime; drug addiction; workplace violence; identity theft; assassination of President Abraham Lincoln; the U.S. National Debt; and countless other ills throughout the World.

Because, as any sane, clear-headed, open-minded, rational-thinking, mature human being knows—those cited above, and countless other yet to be identified Russian-colluded curses and plagues against humankind, **are clearly and indisputably caused by and the responsibility of President Trump, and his incessant "Make America Great Again" endeavor!**

And, those that fail to understand and acknowledge this factually-defendable reality are clearly, plainly, and simply, among the many "despicable deplorables" who are hell-bent to roadblock continuation of Past-President Obama's "Transformation (destruction) of America" agenda. A shameful legacy the radical-left unrelentingly defends and promotes to this day.

However, all is not lost, for the solution is clear and simple. Replace President Trump with a "deep state" created Obama/Clinton clone that "fake news media" will 24/7 support, and other radical-left parties will unrelentingly worship. And then—all will be well once again!

But, good judgement strongly suggests that now is a good place to halt this particular writing. Before inadvertently revealing yet another of my numerous personal short-falls—such as, the occasional use of just a trace of often difficult to recognize cynicism and sarcasm to communicate very serious concerns about truly important issues.

= = =

"Sometimes by losing a battle you find a new way to win the war."
— *Donald J. Trump (1946-), 45th U.S. President.*

"I've missed more than 9000 shots in my career. I've lost almost 300 games. 26 times, I've been trusted to take the game winning shot and missed. I've failed over and over and over again in my life. And that is why I succeed." — *Michael Jordan (1963-), American former professional basketball player; principal owner and chairman of Charlotte Hornets of National Basketball Association.*

"I hated every minute of training, but I said, 'Don't quit. Suffer now and live the rest of your life as a champion." — *Muhammad Ali (1942-2016), American professional boxer; activist; philanthropist; regarded as one of greatest boxers and sports figures of all time.*

A Special Message to Past-President Obama

"The best way to not feel hopeless is to get up and do something. Don't wait for good things to happen to you. If you go out and make some good things happen, you will fill the world with hope, you will fill yourself with hope." — *Barack Obama (1961-), 44th U.S. President.*

[Foreword: Considering that I and countless millions of others worldwide have, as of this writing, so far been exposed to nothing less than an unrelenting 24/7 hammering of anti-Trump and anti-Conservative propaganda since our nation's 2016 Elections . . . it seems clearly fitting to share a bit of differing perspective by way of the following open letter.

It seems important to note that the general content of this letter has in large measure also been previously communicated by way of various social media posts; personal blog site articles and commentary; as well as e-mails and formal letters sent to President Obama's attention.]

Dear Mr. President,

About the time you and First Lady Michelle were poised to enter the White House to "serve" we-the-people, your combined net-worth was reportedly about $1.3 million. A nest egg that has thereafter (as of this writing) reportedly grown to an estimated $40 million to $75 million, depending on the information source.

A net-worth that of course does not yet include a $65 million joint book deal you have since reportedly signed, nor the actual value of a multi-million dollar Obama-Netflix production deal, which was no doubt aided along by one of Netflix's new board members, Susan Rice, who "served" as your national security advisor. You know, the same Susan Rice who took the fall for you and Secretary of State Clinton by appearing on an array of Sunday talk shows in 2012, as she blatantly lied to we-the-people about the "terrorist massacre" carried out on our U.S. diplomatic compound in Benghazi, Libya (i.e., blaming the deadly attack instead on reaction to an internet video).

And, of course, the above wealth-estimates do not include the over $200,000 per year past-president lifetime pension; security services; and other U.S. taxpayer-funded perks you and your family are also recipient of. Overall, according to data collected by Analytics@American, an online business analytics program from American University, you and Michelle could very well amass an estimated $242.5 million or more during your "post-presidency."

But, now in your retirement days, what are you the to a growing many the "ex-liar in chief"; the racially-biased "divider in chief"; the in many ways demonstrated enemy-within of our U.S. Constitution, borders, common-language English, and common-culture founded on Judeo-Christian values, etc., now doing with your leisure time? Well, you can be assured you have not as of this writing been striving to protect and preserve our Constitutional Republic for the benefit of present and future generations of Americans!

No, you have not been using your oratory skills, wealth, or other resources to help the current administration clean-up the social and economic mess left by you and others. For, much to the contrary, you have once again been out on the campaign trail, spreading the same old nation-destructive agenda through the same old pack of lies and same old tools of deception.

And, just in case you and others have a little difficulty recalling how the Obama agenda of racially-charged lies and deception was earlier and remains packaged, for consumption by your target audience of the "always offended" and "forever victims" — below is a snapshot from the past, from your "Change We Can Believe In" pitch.

These of course being but a few of the many, historically-demonstrated False and Deceptive Declarations of Candidate/U.S. President Barack Hussein Obama:

"We have a choice in this country. We can accept a politics that breeds division and conflict and cynicism . . . That is one option. Or, at this moment, in this election, we can come together and say, 'Not this time' . . . ."

"The first thing I will do as President will be to reverse the illegal and unconstitutional aspects of the Patriot Act, with the stroke of my pen."

". . . that means no more illegal wiretapping of American citizens."

"I don't want to pit Red America against Blue America. I want to be the president of the United States of America."

". . . I taught the Constitution for ten years, I believe in the Constitution, and I will obey the Constitution of the United States. We're not goanna use 'signing statements' as a way of doing an end-run around Congress."

"I pledge to cut the deficit we inherited in half by the end of my first term in office."

"I will sign a universal health-care bill into law by the end of my first term as president that will cover every American and cut the cost of a typical family's premium by up to $2,500 a year."

"I, Barack Hussein Obama, do solemnly swear that I will execute the office of president of the United States faithfully, and will to the best of my ability, preserve, protect, and defend the constitution of the United States."

"My administration is committed to creating an unprecedented level of openness in government."

". . . IRS targeting of political dissidents had "not even a smidgen of corruption".

"If you like your doctor, you will be able to keep your doctor. Period. If you like your health care plan, you will be able to keep your health care plan. Period. No one will take it away. No matter what."

". . . I believe in the Second Amendment, I believe in people's lawful right to bear arms, I will not take your shotgun away, I will not take your rifle away . . . ."

"If you've got a business — you didn't build that. Somebody else made that happen."

". . . U.S. will "do what we must" to stop Iran getting nuclear weapons."

And, then there is the March 2012 "hot microphone incident" at your joint press opportunity with then-Russian President Dmitri Medvedev prior to a global nuclear security summit in Seoul, South Korea, that picked up you whispering to Medvedev that you would have *"more flexibility"* to negotiate on issues like missile defense after the 2012 election (i.e., during your second term).

Therefore, in closing, please note that life entails many indisputable realities, such as: (1.) it is difficult to impossible to eat a bowling ball; (2.) from an on-Earth perspective, the sun comes up in the East; and (3.) unfortunately for our country, you and Michelle have turned out to be among America's worst nightmares. And, one that just keeps on and keeps on hanging around, spreading your nation-dividing, nation-destructive venom; one that won't just go-away!

Please also consider that you had your eight-year shot at "transforming" our country into the devastating social and economic mess we are now struggling to recover from. So, please have the decency of heart and mind, and concern for the well-being of present and future generations of Americans, to just zip your arrogant, self-serving, oratorical-gifted lips; go back to your home in the crime-ridden, gun-controlled, city of Chicago; and bask in the good fortune you accumulated while you were so-called "serving" we-the-people."

Sincerely,

William James Moore - *(on behalf of myself and likeminded others)*

= = =

"A Constitution of Government once changed from Freedom, can never be restored. Liberty, once lost, is lost forever." – *John Adams (1735-1826), 2nd U.S. President; a U.S. Founding Father.*

Political Correctness

> *"I think the big problem this country has is being politically correct. I've been challenged by so many people, and I don't frankly have time for total political correctness. And to be honest with you, this country doesn't have time either."*
>
> — *Donald J. Trump (1946-), 45th U.S. President.*

As Albert Einstein long ago noted, "Political Correctness" has truly gone mad. And in recent years has become more and more used as a weapon of the radical political-left in unrelenting efforts to destroy our freedom of speech; our right to offend and be offended; and ultimately our U.S. Constitution, borders, common-language English, and common-culture founded on Judeo-Christian Values.

As commonly officially-defined, **Political Correctness** is *"the avoidance, often taken to extremes, of forms of expression or action that are perceived to exclude, marginalize, or insult groups of people who are socially disadvantaged or discriminated against."*

Therefore, in keeping with above definition, for one to be **Politically Correct** requires one to *"conform to a belief that language and practices which could offend political sensibilities (as in matter of sex, race, etc.) should be eliminated."*

However, after getting past the ever-growing emotional hissy-fit of certain among us about "being offended," and after stripping Political Correctness of its Trojan-horse camouflage, those among us still hanging on to some resemblance of sanity recognize Political Correctness to actually be nothing less than intentional or ignorant *"denial of truth, common sense, and reality"*!

Or, as an Unknown Author once more fittingly defined, *"A doctrine, fostered by a delusional, illogical minority, and rabidly promoted by an unscrupulous mainstream media, which holds forth the proposition that it is entirely possible to pick up a turd by the clean end."*

Or, as George Carlin even more aptly explained: *"Political Correctness is fascism pretending to be manners."* And, as he so insightfully further elaborated: *"Political Correctness is America's newest form of intolerance, and it is especially pernicious because it comes disguised as tolerance. It presents itself as fairness, yet attempts to restrict and control people's language with strict codes and rigid rules. I'm not sure silencing people or forcing them to alter their speech is the best method for solving problems that go much deeper than speech."*

=   =   =

"To Run" or "Not to Run" for U.S. President?

"Democracy is being allowed to vote for the candidate you dislike the least." — Robert Byrne (1930-2016), American author; Billiard Congress of America Hall of Fame instructor of pool and carom billiards.

"The ultimate value of transparency is that voters get to see who is for your and who is against you and what their investment is. It makes it so they get to see who owns you." — Thomas Davis (1814-1845), Irish writer; chief organizer of the Young Ireland movement.

Our 2020 U.S. Presidential Election is scheduled for Tuesday, November 3, 2020 — a little more than about 20 months from this writing! And, it seems every day we hear of someone announcing, or getting ready to announce their candidacy.

Of course the one to beat—President Trump, whom will by then be age 74. However, if meant for me to still be around and above ground, so-to-speak, at that time, I won't be "all that much older than he." So, have been giving some thought about possibly making a run myself. Driven of course by—you know—an unequaled and unrelenting craving to "serve the people."

As well as by the fact that, after years of effort and planning, I have come up with a for certain "sure win" six-point campaign platform that would truly be a shame to let go to waste!

However, at this point, I'm already running into some potentially show-stopping concerns, none the least being "funding issues." For example, according to a reporting by The Washington Post, the final price tag for the 2016 election was about $6.5 billion, for the presidential and congressional elections combined. The presidential contest—primaries and all—accounted for some $2.4 billion of that total. From which, Clinton's unsuccessful campaign ($768 million in spending) outspent Trump's successful one (of $398 million) by nearly 2 to 1. So, any way I dice and slice it, history and logic says I'm presently short somewhere between about $400 million to $800 million. A daunting challenge to say the least!

But, back to my earlier mentioned "sure win" campaign platform, as summarized below:

(1.) Convincingly promise "more free stuff" from the public treasury than promised by President Trump and all other candidates combined;

(2.) Convincingly demonstrate that I hate President Trump and America "much more than" the combined hatred of all other presidential candidates;

(3.) Convincingly swear that I am not a "traditional Democrat," but rather, a "much more" dyed-in-the-wool progressively-savvy "socialist-democrat" than all other candidates combined. Without ever explaining or admitting, of course, that world history shows that "socialism" is a stepping stone to "communism";

(4.) Convincingly promise to, on day one of my presidency, issue an Executive Order establishing the U.S. as a "Sanctuary Nation," with open (not effectively secured/controlled) borders, for all illegal aliens who: still hold allegiance to their failed homeland of origin; refuse to learn "and use" the U.S. common-language English; refuse to assimilate the U.S. common-culture founded on Judeo-Christian values; overwhelm U.S. schools, hospitals, law enforcement, and other infrastructure; abuse and bankrupt the U.S. welfare system; etc., etc.—and, most importantly, always faithfully and consistently vote for all socialist-democrat candidates, or better yet, candidates that promise to replace our U.S. Constitution with life and liberty-destroying Sharia Law;

(5.)   With as-needed fist-pounding, screaming, screeching, shouting, and verbal utterances of the "F" word and other profanity, convincingly make a commitment to purge the U.S. of "all" legal-citizen-owned weapons, as well as "all" persons determined through democrat-socialist party opinion and/or prime time news media coverage, to be racist, sexist, homophobic, xenophobic, Islamaphobic, and/or other-phobic, in addition to those inclined to "offend" others, be not politically correct, and/or be seekers and respecters of truth, fact, and reality;

(6.) And, last but not least, convincingly promise to, within the first 100 days of defeating the Trump Presidency, purge all aspects of the federal government of any and all traces of the prior Trump Administration.   This being an especially popular commitment, especially with the "Deep State" which will ultimately be willfully instrumental in swiftly carrying it out.

While a growing many of the competition no doubt strive to "copycat" the above truly original platform elements, it's now back to pondering the aforementioned campaign "funding issues."   Not for sure why, but as the pressure mounts to make a decision whether to go for it or not, the potential need to one day have to consider threats of "colluding" keeps coming to mind, along with the hazards associated with other random terms and names, such as, the Clinton Foundation, George Soros, etc.

Oh well, at least by identifying as a democrat-socialist, fair and balanced media coverage shouldn't be an issue. Nor, should a "personal background check" be needed or of any importance — which would otherwise for me be a for certain political nail-in-the-coffin show-stopper, so-to-speak!

But, again, after it is all said and done, the bottom line is that it's all about "personal sacrifice" and "serving the people"!

And, never, never, never a smidgen about the craving of power and personal gain!

= = =

"Big corporations and the richest 1% of Americans have poured hundreds of millions of dollars into Washington, purchasing enormous political influence and drowning out the voice of average Americans" — *Robert Reich (1946-), American political commentator; professor; author; U.S. Secretary of Labor from 1993-1997.*

"I will tell you that our system is broken. I give to many people, I give to everybody, when they call I give, and you know what? When I need something from them, two years, three years later, I call, they are there for me." — *Donald Trump (1946-), [from campaign speech as a U.S. Presidential candidate]; as of 2016, 45th U.S. President.*

"Let only individuals contribute — with sensible limits per election. Otherwise, we are well on our way to ensuring that a government of the moneyed, by the moneyed, and for the moneyed shall not perish from the earth." — Warren Buffett (1930-), American business magnate; investor; speaker, philanthropist; Chairman and CEO of Berkshire Hathaway.

Ever-Growing Arsenal of the Radical Political-Left

"Whoever would overthrow the liberty of a nation must begin by subduing the freeness of speech." — *Benjamin Franklin (1706-1790), one of U.S. Founding Fathers; American polymath; author; printer; scientist; inventor; statesman; humorist; diplomat, freemason.*

The Radical Political-Left's U.S./liberty-destroying arsenal continues to be ever-growing. Among their latest sought after weapons at the time of this writing—the voting age lowered to 16.

You know . . . that once assumed "impervious" and "knowing-it-all" age, when I (and likely a sizable number of others) were actually consumed with terminal cluelessness and an overabundance of often publicly revealed irresponsibility.

That exceptionally hormone-driven stage of youth; "five-years-younger-than" the golden age of 21, which state after state and city after city still today declare to be the mature enough age to then purchase tobacco products, alcoholic beverages, or a rifle or pistol, etc.

And, even two years younger than the age permitted to join the military without parental consent.

Yes, in keeping with the Radical-Left's unrelenting battle for "votes" to preserve positions of self-serving power, influence, and control—we must now add the "Voting Age of 16" to their already over bloated vote-assuring arsenal.

A Radical-Left sustaining arsenal already including such weapons as, to cite but a few: open borders, uncontrolled immigration, illegal alien drivers permits, political correctness (denial of truth), racist-labeling, victimhood, deserving, entitlement without contribution, income inequality, climate change, socialism/communism, un-inclusiveness, counselor staffed safe-spaces for offended youth, taxpayer funded pet puppies/kittens for over-anxious students, liberal-biased educational institutions, liberal-biased news media, liberal-biased "deep state" of Washington DC career bureaucrats, and the anti-conservative policies and blocking algorithms of Google, Facebook, Twitter, etc. Not to mention the host of taxpayer funded "Freebees," such as: food, clothing, housing, healthcare, transportation, smartphones, Internet access, legal representation, etc.

Therefore, ranking most high on the scale of self-destructive delusion and irresponsibility would be any move on the part of America's so-called adults in the room, to turn the fate of our country over to our nation's immature youth, by way of our nation's elections or otherwise.

To generations of youth who, for example, in unsettling numbers, actively engage in shouting down the free speech and rightful expression of others who they disagree with. As many have been led to believe that the preservation of their liberty and freedom rests with fascism, socialism, and communism.

While growing numbers march in the streets demanding delusional protection from "climate change" — as in ignorance they turn their heads away from the real threats posed by nuclear weapons, radical-militant Islam, Sharia law, female genital mutilation, socialism, communism, the anti-U.S. governments of Iran and North Korea, corruption in our U.S. government, and liberal-biased educational institutions that fail to help prepare America's youth for the realities of life.

Realities including, for example, the fact that criminals, terrorists, and others hell-bent to do harm to others could care less about laws, gun-free zone signs, or about offending someone. As well as other inescapable realities, such as, nothing is ever truly "Free" — because someone, somewhere, somehow, at some point in time, must ultimately do the "paying" . . . even for one's precious liberty and freedom, now too often abused and dangerously taken for granted.

It seems Abraham Lincoln was unsettlingly prophetic when reportedly stating, *"America will never be destroyed from the outside. If we falter and lose our freedoms, it will be because we destroyed ourselves."*

= = =

"We must speak our minds openly, debate our disagreements honestly, but always pursue solidarity."
— Donald J. Trump (1946-), 45th U.S. President.

"One of the key problems today is that politics is such a disgrace, good people don't go into government."
— Donald J. Trump (1946-), 45th U.S. President.

"When America is united, America is totally unstoppable."
— Donald J. Trump (1946-), 45th U.S. President.

The Deafening Silence of Benign Neglect

Benign neglect is commonly considered an *"attitude or policy of ignoring an often delicate or undesirable situation that one is held to be responsible for dealing with."*

We would have zero tolerance for any predictable natural disaster—threatening untold thousands (possibly millions) of us—being treated with the "deafening silence of benign neglect."

Yet, regarding nuclear threats posed by the radical U.S.-hating regimes of Iran and North Korea, many among us continue to bury our heads in ignorance, apathy, and complacency. Seeking refuge in a suicidal fantasy land of denial, enabled in large measure by irresponsible news/social media, politicians, and others, absorbed in the relatively petty whims of those hell-bent to be "offended" about something. Nevertheless, and at risk of interfering with some "Internet gone viral" posting of the moment, what follows is a much past-due historical reality-check worth pondering.

In August 1945 (during final stages of World War II), the U.S. dropped atomic bombs on the Japanese cities of Hiroshima and Nagasaki. The (so far) first and only use of nuclear weapons in wartime. Together these two bombings killed an estimated 150,000 to 250,000 people, mostly civilians. About half the deaths occurred the day of bombing. The other half, some 75,000 to 125,000, over the following months, as a result of burns, radiation sickness, and related injuries and illness. About 132 pounds of highly-enriched uranium was used in the bomb released over Hiroshima, Japan's seventh largest city at that time. It destroyed about 90 percent of the city. About 17 pounds of plutonium-239 was used in the explosive charge of the bomb dropped 3 days later on Nagasaki. Within about 6 years after these horrific bombings, atomic weapon devices were being tested which had explosive forces about <u>a thousand times greater</u>.

Fast-forwarding to more recent times—on January 30, 2018, U.S. CIA Director, Mike Pompeo, warned that North Korea could have a nuclear weapon capable of striking the United States within **"a handful of months."** A reality that all our "sanctuary cities/states," and taxpayer-funded "safe spaces" in our schools, etc., will not make go away. A reality we had better soon, seriously, and rationally start having very public national discussion about.

Because, in the final analysis, the responsibility for our national security ultimately rests with "we the people," through our elected U.S. President and Congressional Representatives.

And, therefore, it is our inescapable duty to make clear to all concerned that we will not—under any circumstances—tolerate those chanting "death to America" to have at their disposal, the means to reap indescribable death and destruction upon us.

There is no longer a road to kick the can down. So, within **"a handful of months"** North Korea must self-eliminate its nuclear arsenal. Or, "we the people"—through our elected President, other government representatives, and military—must be prepared, able, and willing to take whatever action necessary to eliminate such threat.

And, should the courage to deal with this inescapable obligation be in need of a booster shot—a source for such may likely be found in the trusting eyes of our nation's young children and grandchildren.

= = =

"When I was a sophomore at USC, I was a socialist, pretty much to the left. But not when I left the university. I quickly got wise. I'd read about what had happened to Russia in 1917 when the Communists took over." — *John Wayne (1907-1979), American actor; filmmaker; Presidential Medal of Freedom recipient.*

Wishful Blaming of "Things"

"The victim mindset dilutes the human potential. By not accepting personal responsibility for our circumstances, we greatly reduce our power to change them." — *Steve Maraboli (1975-), Internet radio commentator; motivational speaker; author.*

What will to some likely forever seem only yesterday—on October 01, 2017 a shooting massacre in Las Vegas took the lives of at least 59 and injured hundreds of others.

And as many struggle to cope with, or strive to erase recall of, that horrific tragedy, we are provided with continuing evidence that truly despicable evil exists in the hearts and minds of some among us.

Such as, the radical Islamic terrorist that used a truck to kill at least 8 and injure many others in New York City on October 31, 2017.

And, more recently, the killer that used a gun to massacre at least 26 and wound some 20 others in a rural Texas church on November 5, 2017 (a tragedy that could have been worse had not a local resident been willing and able to use his personal gun to confront the killer).

As truly terrible that these within-our-borders tragedies are, such are but a relative few of the countless carried out worldwide, past, present. And, no words can fittingly communicate the heinous nature of such barbaric assaults against humankind, nor relate the resulting pain, suffering, and other associated trauma.

Many among us hopelessly strive and struggle to understand "why" anyone is capable of and chooses to carry out such unspeakable acts. Nonetheless, it just possibly might be a natural blessing that most of us continue to be frustrated by our failure to grasp such understanding.

For, to truly understand such unspeakable behaviors would seem to require being able to make sense out of that which truly makes no sense. An understanding that might well ultimately require a heart and mind in dangerous likeness to those who harbor and carry out the very despicable evils that we are puzzled and threatened by.

Therefore, possibly a more realistic response to such evil would be to accept that it does exist; that some among us will attempt or succeed in carrying out acts of evil; and therefore take realistic steps to prevent and defend against such.

Beginning with a discontinuance of efforts to disarm law abiding citizens and otherwise restrict our rights and ability to defend ourselves. And, by also ceasing to pretend that such acts of evil are harbored, planned, and executed by "things" (guns, knives, cars, trucks, aircraft, explosives, fertilizer, etc.), rather than by unhinged "people".

Likewise, in realistically focusing on "evil's reality" and "people behavior" versus "things" — possibly we, the mainstream media, and our government representatives and leaders, can soon, rather than too late, include a fitting level of responsible attention to our nation-wide and rapidly growing "addictive drugs" epidemic.

Because, "people" (not "things") abusing opioids and other legal and illegal addictive drugs now represent the leading cause of injury related death in the United States. Exceeding injury related deaths from use of cars and guns!

For example, during the timeframe of 2002-2016, over 500,000 people in the U.S. died from drug overdoses. An average of over 35,000 per year, or about 1 drug overdose death every 15 minutes! With a more recent February 22, 2019 U.S. News report citing that opioid overdose deaths in the United States have quadrupled in the last two decades! And, National Institute on Drug Abuse (NIH) statistics, updated in January 2019, showing that more than 70,200 Americans died from drug overdoses in 2017, including illicit drugs and prescription opioids — a two-fold increase in just one decade!

And, it is a rapidly growing reality that someone in each of our respective families has been or will be touched by the devastation of drug abuse, dependency, and addiction. Or that our families know of someone who has, or likely will be!

= = =

"We live in a culture of blame. People will blame anyone or anything for their misery sooner than take the responsibility to own it and make it better." — Dr. Henry Cloud (1956-), American Christian self-help author; Dr. John Townsend (1952-), American Christian self-help author.

Hope Survives Age-Old Struggle of Good vs Evil

> *"I am in politics because of the conflict between good and evil, and I believe that in the end good will triumph."* – Margaret Thatcher (1925-2013), Prime Minister of United Kingdom, 1979-1990.

The various massacres and other atrocities suffered within America's borders and elsewhere around the World are painful reminders that, in a world of much good, there also exists considerable evil.

Nevertheless, from heartbreaking struggle with evil, "good" can be the ultimate victor and "hope" a crucial survivor. As demonstrated by the many, from all walks of life, who unfailingly confront evil's despicable works. For example, the countless and often unnamed: first responders; law enforcement; medical professionals; military personnel, and an array of others. People giving of themselves through often heroic acts of courage and self-sacrifice. Invaluable demonstrations of true caring for fellow human beings. Unfortunately, for many the triumph of "good" over "evil" can be long coming, or never realized. Often from ignorance, apathy, complacency, denial, greed, and fear, of those having the means for life circumstances to be otherwise.

As evidenced, for example, by millions massacred not so long ago at the hand of Hitler's regime, as too many nations for too long turned their heads away. And, more recently, as demonstrated by millions trapped in the menacing jaws of barbaric regimes such as North Korea, and countless others worldwide deprived of life, liberty, and pursuit of happiness.

While some among us take for granted, and/or choose to show disrespect for, our precious liberty and freedom and nation's symbols of same.

The faces of evil are many and often masked. However, regardless of where, when, and how revealed — evil originates not in "things" (knives, guns, explosives, car-bombs, hijacked-aircraft, etc.), but in the hearts and minds of humankind. In "intent" and "choices."

And, while fortunately a relative few have the "intent" and "choose" to do so — every able body human being has the ability to harm others. But, rather than acknowledging and trying to constructively deal with these aspects of human nature, many prefer to deny or ignore such and futilely continue to blame human failings on "things." A historically demonstrated self-destructive path. As evidenced, for example, by related circumstances playing out in Great Britain. Where, after being disarmed, law enforcement personnel and law abiding citizens are now often essentially defenseless against armed terrorists and other criminal elements. Including those reportedly carrying out epidemic levels of horrifying attacks with "knives" and "acids." Other reminders that the distracting focus on "things" fails to meaningfully address the "evil intent" in the hearts and minds of some. And that those hell-bent to inflict cruelty upon others, have at their disposal an essentially limitless array of ways and means.

The "good vs evil" struggle is an age-old human condition. And, as historically the case, the victor between these two conflicting sides of humankind will likely always be—**the one we choose to nurture the most**, as individuals and as a nation.

Therein likely rests the prospects for hope's survival—and of our ultimate fate and that of future generations.

= = =

"I would rather be a little nobody, than to be an evil somebody." — *Abraham Lincoln (1809-1865), 16th U.S. President.*

"Keep your values positive because your values become your destiny." — *Mahatma Gandhi (1869-1948), Indian activist; leader of Indian independence movement against British colonial rule.*

"What truly matters is not which party controls our government, but whether our government is controlled by the people. January 20th 2017, will be remembered as the day the people became the rulers of this nation again. The forgotten men and women will be forgotten no longer. Everyone is listening to you." — Donald J. Trump (1946-), 45th U.S. President.

Life's Inescapable Realities

"The great enemy of the truth is very often not the lie, deliberate, contrived and dishonest, but the myth, persistent, persuasive, and unrealistic." — *John F. Kennedy (1917-1963), 35th U.S. President.*

Along with blessings experienced by a countless many, come a number of life's inescapable realities.

Such as, to note but a few: some among us pay taxes, others do not; there is no such thing as "free" (someone, somewhere, at some point, pays); death eventually applies to all; the Sun comes up in the East; you can't eat a bowling ball (at least not in its intended-for-use form); life is not fair; freedom of speech does not only apply to what you or I agree with, but also the views of others; only those who successfully win the battle against evil and oppression will have the opportunity to realize the inalienable (God-given) rights to life, liberty, and pursuit of happiness; and, both our "voting" and "not voting" have truly serious, long-lasting, and otherwise profound consequences.

Yes, the conduct (good, bad, or indifferent) of our local, state, and federal government is ultimately the consequence of votes cast, or not cast, by "we the people" — past, present, and future.

A reality not erasable by any amount of wrongly assigned blame/credit. For, in our U.S. constitutional republic, it is our votes or lack thereof that determine who will be granted positions of governmental power and influence over our lives and livelihood. An awesome extent of power and influence our country's Founding Fathers wisely intended to be duly limited and held in check. By way of the Bill of Rights and other liberty recognizing provisions of our very unique and most precious U.S. Constitution — our firewall against tyranny — our safeguard against cruel or oppressive government or rule.

And, for those who continue to maintain that our votes don't matter, note that our recently completed 2018 midterm elections reportedly entailed campaign spending totaling well over a staggering $5 billion. An unthinkable expenditure that of course does not include the untold millions upon millions of untraceable dollars (so-called "dark money"). All spent in a grueling battle for our votes — in an unrelenting struggle for positions of power and influence within our government. Votes, and lack of votes, that truly have consequences!

For, in the end, it will be our votes and failure to vote that determine, for example:

- whether our liberty-sustaining U.S. Constitution survives, or is replaced by life/liberty-destroying Sharia Law or other cruel and oppressive rule;

- whether our nation's foundation blocks of secured borders, common language-English, and common culture founded on Judeo-Christian values, continue to survive, or are destroyed by irresponsible immigration policies;

- whether we have a free-enterprise economic system that promotes continued growth, prosperity, innovation, individual opportunity, and security, or suffer the liberty-destructive ravages of socialism and communism;

- whether our ever-growing and out-of-control $22 trillion national debt is responsibly dealt with, or we self-destruct from continued out-of-control government spending;

- whether our educational institutions teach truth and help prepare our nation's youth to responsibly deal with the realities of life, or continues to condition them to scramble for the false security of a taxpayer-funded "safe space" and delusional comfort of an "anxiety-relieving kitten/puppy," at the first encounter with a view not aligned with that of their own;

- whether we accept the reality of "limited resources," or self-destruct under the delusion that the cost of so-called "free" food, clothing, housing, education, transportation, entertainment, legal services, smart phones, and other wants and needs, will somehow be paid for by the "tooth fairy" or some other "elusive them."

- whether we recognize and embrace "truth" and "reality" and encourage unity, or continue to self-destruct under the delusions of "political correctness (i.e., denial of truth)" and at the hand of "identity politics" and "divide and conquer" agendas;

And, by no means the last nor least --- whether our nation is constructively supported by an election process of integrity, inputted by informed and responsible voters, or suffers the liberty threatening consequences of a system contaminated by input of non-U.S. citizens, sabotage by foreign governments, and/or from the ignorance, apathy, complacency, denial, and greed, of we U.S. citizens.

= = =

"Freedom of speech and thought matters, especially when it is speech and thought with which we disagree. The moment the majority decides to destroy people for engaging in thought it dislikes, thought crime becomes a reality." — Ben Shapiro (1984-), American conservative political commentator; writer; lawyer.

"Once Upon a Time"

"Government is not a solution to our problem, government is the problem." – Ronald Reagan (1911-2004), 40th U.S. President.

"Once upon a time" some very wise and courageous men and women fled a county of tyranny, and in another land established an envy-of-the-world constitutional republic of unequaled liberty and opportunity (our USA), after at heavy sacrifice first defeating the military of their once cruel and oppressive king. That time was long ago.

"Once upon a time" people legally immigrated to this best hope for humankind; proudly took the initiative to become lawful U.S. citizens;   learned and used its common-language English; assimilated its common-culture founded on Judeo-Christian values; worked hard to make it an even better place for their children and grandchildren; and successfully defended it time and again against threats foreign and domestic. That time still exists for millions of people who respect America's constitution, laws, borders, language, and culture.

"Once upon a time" illegal aliens began: invading this best hope for humankind; seeking out sanctuary states and cities where U.S. citizenship is not needed in order to pillage the public treasury; refusing to learn and use our common-language English; refusing to assimilate our common-culture founded on Judeo-Christian values; disrespecting our U.S. Flag and the constitutional republic it represents; and, rather than working to help build upon America's many successes, choosing to contaminate our country with anti-American cultures, crime, corruption, and otherwise liberty-destroying social decay, in likeness to the failed nations from which they came. That time began many years ago, still exists, and continues to worsen.

"Once upon a time" generations of relatively spoiled and world/U.S. history-ignorant citizens, consumed with self-destructive apathy, complacency, denial, and greed, found that they could get so-called "free stuff" from the public treasury, by electing representatives who would accommodate their self-serving desires. As corrupt and power-craving politicians likewise found their positions self-serving indulgence could be seemingly life-time secured by promising their constituents endless outpourings of so-called "free stuff" from the public treasury. Even if doing so required running our nation into unsustainable, liberty-destroying debt. That time began years ago, still exist, and is rapidly worsening at a critical rate.

"Once upon a time" our country's foreign and domestic enemies realized that they could eventually destroy this best hope for humankind without firing a shot (so to speak). By infiltrating our news media, and administration of our schools/colleges/universities, and our government, with those who unrelentingly support, through intent or ignorance, anti-American/anti-U.S. Constitution ideology. That time was long ago, still exists, and is rapidly worsening at a critical pace. And has and continues to contaminate an ever-growing critical mass of legal and illegal voters who have loaded, and continue to load, the elected and appointed positions of power within our government with individuals having radical-left, socialist, communist, radical-Islamic, and other anti-American/anti-U.S. Constitution aims.

And, we so-called adults in the room had damn well better wake up, and by way of our votes and other respective ways and means, start openly and constructively confronting and combatting the nation-destructive insanity taking place all around us!

Otherwise, there will shamefully be another **"once upon a time"**!

A time when our children and grandchildren will suffer unthinkable life and liberty threatening hardship! As they, at great sacrifice, are called upon to strive, struggle, and fight to salvage the precious liberty that we let others chip, chip, chip away and ultimately destroy before our eyes. As we and others before us have irresponsibly basked in self-destructive apathy, complacency, denial, and greed. And have likewise wallowed in the lunacy-founded, counter-productive "fear of offending" someone—especially those who, through intent or ignorance, have been and continue to be hell-bent to deny us and others the inalienable (God-given) rights to life, liberty, and pursuit of happiness.

= = =

"Germany was beaten after World War I, but it didn't take long for it to rise again as a much more malignant threat. The end of World War II was not a compromise; it was to come about from the total annihilation of the enemies' ability and will to make war." — Monica Crowley (1968-), American political commentator; lobbyist; Fox News contributor, 1996-2017.

The Age of Personal Responsibility?

"When people ae desperate or wealthy, they turn to socialism; only when they have no other alternative do they embrace the free market. After all, lies about guaranteed security are far more seductive than lectures about personal responsibility." — Ben Shapiro (1984-), American conservative political commentator; writer; lawyer.

The March 05, 2019 edition of our local newspaper included an informative front page article titled, "City makes tobacco 21 more restrictive." In which it was explained that on March 04 our City Commissioners voted 3-1 to eliminate exemptions in an ordinance that made it illegal for most people under 21 to buy tobacco or vaping liquid.

Like many other communities, adding but another chapter, so-to-speak, to the seemingly never ending struggle to define to the satisfaction of all, the "age of personal responsibility."

A no doubt well-intentioned struggle by all concerned, that none the less appears to have to date unduly discounted or minimized some meaningful perspectives, such as:

(1.) Many of our nation's now so-called adults have the view that adulthood starts at 18 and that city ordinances, etc., should not take away a law-abiding adult's rights;

(2.) The Twenty-sixth Amendment prohibits the federal government from using age as a reason for denying law-abiding citizens, at least 18 years old, their right to vote;

(3.) The U.S. permits our law-abiding youth to join the military at age 18 (and at age 17 with parental consent);

(4.) The State of Kansas, for example, allows our youth, after reaching age 15 and having held an instruction permit at least one year, to apply for a restricted driver's license; and at age 16 and a half to be issued a full license; and without parental consent take on the responsibilities of marriage at age 18.

(5.) The minimum age for marriage in the U.S. is set by each state. For all states except two, a couple may marry without the requirement for parental consent when both are 18 years of age or older. In Nebraska, both must be over 19, and in Mississippi, over 21. In most states, couples are allowed to marry at a younger age with the consent of both parents or with judicial consent; with the minimum age for marriage when all exemptions are taken into account varying from state to state.

Some seem to find logic and peace of mind in our law-abiding youth being "old enough" to drive a potentially deadly vehicle; vote in our nation's elections; be put in harm's way in our military; and get married—but not "old enough" to purchase and/or possess, for example, a hand gun, rifle, alcoholic drinks, or tobacco products.

Some feel otherwise. Some continue to ponder whether there truly is a specific age (or ever), when many among us become able and willing to demonstrate good judgement in making life's many choices, especially those affecting not only one's self, but also others.

Personally, I have found that many of my most poor judgements were not carried out during my teens, but rather, after reaching so-called adulthood. And, looking around, it seems clear that my experience is by no measure uncommon.

Therefore, somewhere in our relatively futile quest to control human behavior, is an often muted cry for common sense to prevail. While recognizing that we are each unique beings, born with unique physical and mental attributes; raised and educated under varying conditions; and exposed to diverse life-circumstances and differing opportunities.

As each of the able minded and able bodied among us must ultimately one day accept and be held accountable for—**"the age of personal responsibility."** That yet elusive age which we will likely long-strive to affix a golden number to.

"And whether a child is born in the urban sprawl of Detroit or the windswept plains of Nebraska, they look up at the same night sky, they fill their heart with the same dreams, and they are infused with the breath of life by the same almighty Creator." – Donald Trump *(1946-), 45th U.S. President.*

Roots of Our Liberty & Coveted "E-Devices"

> *"It has been said that democracy is the worst form of government except all those other forms that have been tried from time to time."*
> —*Winston Churchill (1874-1965), Prime Minister of the United Kingdom, 1940-1945; led Britain to victory in World War II.*

What is of course not a newsflash to the right-minded among us—the smartphone, iPad, E-Tablet, PC, laptop, wide-screen TV, Xbox, and countless supporting apps, etc., did not originate in dictator-ruled North Korea; or communist China, Russia, and Cuba.

Or in Islam-ruled Iran, Iraq, and Saudi Arabia; war-torn Syria; or in a radical-Islamic caliphate.

Nor in the now before-our-eyes self-destructing Venezuela or in a long list of other socialist-failed nations.

Nor, did an exceptionally generous tooth fairy leave us with these seemingly "now-can't-do-without" devices — these now essentially "additional body-parts" — these now entrenched "means of communications and entertainment" — these in many cases increasingly business and government "essential technologies."

No, very much to the contrary. Instead, such technology came about through people having the opportunity to express and pursue their creativity and for-profit economic endeavors. People fortunate to live in a unique Constitutional Republic (the USA) that embraces the inalienable (God-given) rights to life, liberty, and pursuit of happiness. Not a guarantee against failure, but the right to seek one's understanding of personal fulfillment.

Rights acknowledged by a first and yet one of its kind U.S. Constitution. A "crucial-to-individual-liberty" constitution originated long ago by exceptionally wise individuals. Persons who not only escaped tyranny and courageously fought for and achieved liberty, but also were determined to preserve it. By putting in place a government "of, by, and for" the people.

A most precious Republic offering a lasting constitutional barrier to the return of tyranny or other oppressive rule over its citizens — a barrier that must, however, be ultimately defended and preserved by "each generation" of Americans.

A Constitutional Republic that is now not only facing an array of new and long-standing "foreign threats," but also that of wide-spread "enemies from within"! Serious "domestic threats" that, most sadly, includes growing numbers within more recent generations of Americans. Individuals who are ignorant of, or have lost-touch with, our country's roots.

Individuals who fail to grasp that our nation, and too-often taken for granted liberty, cannot survive without protecting and preserving our U.S. Constitution; borders, common-language English; common-culture founded on Judeo-Christian values, and market-driven economy.

Individuals who by way of their votes and/or other nation-destructive behaviors, are now filling seats within our local, state, and federal government with persons openly or covertly aligned with socialism, communism, radical-Islam, Sharia-law, or other anti-American ideology.

Liberty-threatening, nation-destructive individuals who are being enabled by other Americans who are consumed with ignorance, apathy, complacency, denial, greed, and counter-productive fear.

Fuelled, distracted, and manipulated by corrupt and politically biased individuals imbedded throughout our education system, news media, and government bureaucracy.

Among life's inescapable realities is our ultimate demise! Should we, through ignorance or intent, continue to choose or otherwise tolerate to be represented, governed, or otherwise controlled by, those who have not assimilated our country's roots and refuse to embrace our U.S. Constitution.

= = =

"Courage is what it takes to stand up and speak; courage is also what it takes to sit down and listen." — Winston Churchill (1874-1965), Prime Minister of the United Kingdom, 1940-1945; led Britain to victory in Second World War.

"Politicians can't manage. All they can do is talk." — Donald J. Trump (1946-), 45th U.S. President.

"We will get our people off of welfare and back to work — rebuilding our country with American hands and American labor." — Donald J. Trump (1946-), 45th U.S. President.

"Socialism states that you owe me something simply because I exist. Capitalism, by contrast, results in a sort of reality-forced altruism: I may not want to help you, I may dislike you, but if I don't give you a product or service you want, I will starve. Voluntary exchange is more moral than forced redistribution." — Ben Shapiro (1984-), American conservative political commentator; writer; lawyer.

"They Alone" — Are Not the Problem or Solution

> *"Elections belong to the people. It's their decision. If they decide to turn their back on the fire and burn their behinds, then they will just have to sit on their blisters."* — *Abraham Lincoln (1809-1865), 16th U.S. President.*
>
> *"Leaders lead but in the end it's the people who deliver."* — *Tony Blair (1953 -), Prime Minister of United Kingdom from 1997-2007.*

Few would likely dispute that the "blame game" is enjoying ever growing popularity far beyond that of serious "solution seeking." Especially in the often brutal world of "politics." And with our country's next general elections now being (at the time of this writing) some twenty months away, ample time seems available to sharpen one's fault-assigning skills.

Yes, our country's next general elections will be held Tuesday, November 3, 2020. At that time, all 435 seats in the U.S. House of Representatives; 34 of the 100 U.S. Senate seats; the office of U.S. President; 13 state and territorial governorships;

and numerous other state and local positions of political power and influence will be contested.

Many will try hard to be responsible voters. Others through ignorance or intent will permit propaganda, irrational thinking, etc., cloud their judgement. While, sadly, some will not participate at all—as millions of enslaved or otherwise oppressed people, worldwide, are denied same crucial liberty-preserving opportunity.

As long-typical of each election cycle—much news reporting, social media chatter, and talk-show broadcasts will be flooded with a mix of critiques. Often emotionally-charged views about both the holders and seekers of political positons. Critiques, some founded in truth and fact; others rooted in agenda driven falsehoods, distortions, and ignorance. Critiques that communications technology helps spread ever faster to millions—many of whom are ill prepared to determine legitimacy and/or how to responsibly handle.

Critiques of "They alone" too often failing to acknowledge a most basic and crucial consideration. That being, the political figures often blamed or praised for everything that (so-to-speak) walks, flies, and breaths—are not elevated to positions of political power and influence by the "tooth fairy." But, rather, by "votes"—whether rational, irrational, informed, uninformed, legal, illegal, or otherwise. Votes that reflect the good, bad, or indifferent mindset of those who cast them. Votes having both short-term and long-term consequences.

Consequences such as our now out-of-control and rapidly growing $22 trillion National Debt. A liberty threatening menace not alone created by self-serving power-seekers and others chosen to represent us within the various branches of our government. But also by the self-destructive apathy, complacency, denial, greed, and counter-productive fears of many among us — often rooted in the age-old lust for so-called "free stuff" to be paid for by "someone else."

World history is cluttered with examples where, to their peril, some generations for too long took liberty and freedom for granted. Lest we succumb to similar fate, we must not "too late" grasp that the source of our nation's real and perceived troubles rests not with "They alone" — but more so within the attitudes and behaviors of "we the people." As do also our nation's many examples of past, present, and further sought greatness.

At ultimate risk of our willingness to embrace reality: nothing less than the opportunity for present and future generations of Americans to continue to experience the inalienable (God-given) rights to life, liberty, and pursuit of happiness.

= = =

"When you open your heart to patriotism, there is no room for prejudice. The Bible tells us, 'How good and pleasant it is when God's people live together in unity'." — Donald J. Trump (1946-), 45th U.S. President.

"It is time to remember that old wisdom our soldiers will never forget: that whether we are black or brown or white, we all bleed the same red blood of patriots, we all enjoy the same glorious freedoms, and we all salute the same great American Flag."

— *Donald J. Trump (1946-), 45th U.S. President.*

AMERICA'S "LUNACY WAGON"

> *"The belief that society benefits from destruction is lunacy."*
> — Walter E. Williams (1936-), American economist; commentator.

There is of course much good in the world. That which is truly worthy of our gratitude and efforts to support and add thereto.

There is also much that is not right. Issues truly justifying our concern and responsible attention—well ahead of those merely involving "being offended" by someone or something. And well ahead of trying to manipulate the Earth's ever-changing climate and undertaking other such exercises in utter futility.

Yes, there is an ever growing list of "very real" and "solvable" matters at which our priority attention and limited resources should be directed.

Such as, the ongoing "failures" of our U.S. Congress to:

(1.) Fund construction of a security wall across our nation's historically-proven to be vulnerable southern border. As same Congress continues to obligate billions upon billions of taxpayer dollars to the care and otherwise handling of the countless illegal aliens that flow into our already dangerously in-debt and liberty-threatened country;

(2.) Pursue and hold accountable all persons involved in the corrupt and lawless efforts to destroy and force from office our duly elected President of the United States, Donald J. Trump;

(3.) Purge our country of dangerous and illegal sanctuary city/state laws, policies, and practices;

(4.) Mandate and enforce states to take reasonable steps (as required by law) to clean voter rolls, implement voter ID, and take other commonsense measures to ensure election integrity;

(5.) Hold Hillary Clinton accountable for the email scandal that violated federal laws and endangered our national security;

(6.) Combat the illegal alien crisis by enforcement of current immigration laws, protecting our borders, and putting an end to unlawful sanctuary policies for illegal aliens;

(7.) Investigate extent of improper cooperation between U.S. government officials and groups funded by George Soros;

(8.) Enforce responsible tax and spend policies that will rein in and ultimately eliminate our county's out of control $22 trillion National Debt.

Now, this writer and likeminded others could choose to spend our truly-uncertain share of the blessing of "life," on ways that possibly could more constructively communicate concern and contempt for our government's irresponsible behavior.

Such as: overwhelming the private and public phones, snail-mail boxes, and e-mail files, of our elected "servants of the people" with voice messages, text messages, and letters of protest. Say nothing about other approaches often used by some to air their respective grievances, such as: public marches, boycotts, disruption of traffic, public harassments, destruction of the business/private property of others, etc. Supplemented of course by much more informed and otherwise responsible voting.

However, it is much more likely that I and likeminded others will continue to spend considerable precious time using social media platforms and Internet websites, etc., to vent frustrations shared personally and by countless others. And, in so doing, contribute to the wealth and otherwise welfare of the creators, owners, and investors of Facebook, Google, and Twitter, etc. As the same extremely liberal-entrenched businesses use their complex algorithm technologies to control who (if any) actually have access to our expressed concerns, as well as when, in what format, and for what end-purpose. Some will also, with likewise questionable results, attempt to constructively communicate their concerns through Public Mind articles in their local newspapers and/or by way of self/professionally published books, etc.

And so, **"America's Lunacy Wagon"** moves on! Pulled by horses named Ignorance, Apathy, Complacency, Denial, Greed, and Fear. With the horses' reins in ever-tightening control of a sinister wagoner (driver) named Deep-State, and trusting support-wagoner named Fake-News. While rapidly approaching a crucial fork in the road—with one path leading to the **Preservation of Liberty**; the other to the **Abyss of Tyranny**.

A **"wagon of lunacy"** overloaded with a mix of politicians, voters, non-voters, and other travelers. Some with familiar names such as, apathy, complacency, denial, greed, fear, clueless, intimidated, overbearing, conservative, moderate, reactionary, liberal, radical, right, left, and political-correct. Some regardless of name, sex, ancestry, or otherwise origin or label—nevertheless craving to in some way make or contribute to a meaningful difference; some with otherwise not well-intentioned aims.

With still others struggling to make some resemblance of sense out of the seemingly unexplainable nation-destructive absurdities of the Radical-Left.

Absurdities such as a multi-millionaire U.S. House of Representatives Speaker, and her supporters on both sides of the isle, road blocking a security wall on our southern border that would help protect U.S. citizens, as she and likeminded others live in the comfort of their gated-communities surrounded by security walls/iron fences/etc., as they in turn vote to fund billions upon billions of taxpayer dollars year after year for the care and handling of "illegal aliens."

Nation/liberty-threatening absurdities of the radical-political left explainable by various reality-based sources yet available for those of us still hanging on to some resemblance of sanity. Sources such as, a New York Times bestseller, titled: *"Liberalism is a Mental Disorder,"* by New York Times bestselling author, Michael Savage.

And, for those who have often struggled in vain to have a rational and unemotional discussion with members of the radical-left, some cautionary wisdom can likewise be found in the following quotation, often attributed to Robert A. Heintein: *"Never try to teach a pig to sing; it wastes your time and it annoys the pig."*

In the final analysis, when all the guns have been **banned**; when all the words have been **censored**; when all the history has been **erased**; and when all the liberties and freedoms have been **denied** — only then will it much too late be realized that, upon reaching the crucial fork in the road . . . **America's Lunacy Wagon** chose the wrong path.

"Strange times are these, in which we live,
Forsooth (indeed);
When young and old are taught in Falsehood's school:--
And the man who dares to tell the truth,
Is called at once a lunatic and fool.

— George Francis Train
(1829-1904), American entrepreneur

A Day Brightened

Recently, self-absorbed me was doing a routine power-walk near our community's High School. A spectacle casual observers might likely describe as "pretend exercise."

Nevertheless, while pausing to tighten a shoe string, I very surprisingly received a day-brightening greeting from a complete stranger. One actually acknowledging my existence; even making eye contact!

And, not just hurriedly scurrying-by as more and more tend to do nowadays, seemingly detached from their surroundings, with heads buried in a smartphone screen, or ears plugged with earbuds, etc.

Yes, while appearing to show up out of nowhere, and although now living life after the tragic loss of a leg, this complete stranger took the time and effort to extend a warm greeting to another unknown.

You know what I mean, that very unique and especially friendly "body-language" that a most handsome male dog, with black and white hair, sporting a reddish collar, and missing a right front leg, uses when wishing to warmly engage with us humans!

Thereafter, without a spoken word being exchanged, this complete stranger chose to accompany me for a couple of city blocks or so, alongside, or nearby. As he cheerfully walked, ran, and romped about, with a demonstrated nature of energy, balance, coordination, confidence, and joyfulness that many of his peers having the benefit of all four legs likely much envied.

And, doing so with an enviable spirit void of even the slightest trappings of self-pity, victimhood, and remorse regarding the horrific injury he had obviously once suffered and the special challenges now faced.

For a special moment in time my attention seemed to depart from my "self-absorbed self" — as I instead focused on this most cheerful canine dealing with life and his world while having only three legs.

I wondered what traumatic experience had taken one of his precious front limbs, and thought about the painful, fearful, and challenging recovery process he had to have likewise dealt with. Questioning whether I would be able to in kind endure similar tragedy, and thereafter have the positive and confident attitude he so enthusiastically exhibited. The answer I kept coming up with — very likely, not.

As this cheerful stranger departed my presence, likely in search of more interesting company, I much hoped that his well-kept appearance indicated that his home was nearby and he would soon safely return thereto.

It seems noteworthy that for the most part cats appear to basically "tolerate" us. While dogs are blessed (possibly burdened) with the capacity for "unconditional affection" for we humans — and in some cases, even for the most undeserving among us.

And, regarding our likewise human capacity for "tolerance" and "unconditional affection" for one another, and for other life-forms we share this Earth with — well . . . that seems to be a work in process with indisputably much room for improvement.

But now back to my "self-absorbed self." To face, or find escape from, the many truly real as well as an array of imagined challenges of our so-called superior human world. While basking at times in a sense of self-assumed "terminal uniqueness" — a no doubt not uncommon human condition likely shared by countless others.

Yes, back to a world of real and imagined victims, oppressors, and defenders of liberty and freedom. A world where many are filled with gratitude, as others are consumed with — what the aforementioned three-legged stranger will forever be incapable of — "self-pity."

= = =

"There are moments of life that we never forget, which brighten and brighten as time steals away." — *James Gates Percival (1795-1856), American poet; surgeon; geologist; born in Berlin.*

"If you are always trying to be normal, you will never know how amazing you can be." — *Maya Angelou (1928-2014), American poet; singer; memoirist; civil rights activist.*

"Life is 10 percent what happens to you and 90 percent how you react to it." — *Charles R. Swindoll (1934-), evangelical Christian pastor; author; educator; founder of 'Insight for Living'.*

Our Constitutional Republic

> *"A [pure] democracy is nothing more than mob rule, where fifty-one percent of the people may take away the rights of the other forty-nine."* — *Thomas Jefferson (1743-1826), 3rd U.S. President; one of U.S. Founding Fathers.*
>
> *"The mob is the mother of tyrants."* — *Diogenes (412BC-323BC), Greek philosopher; one of the founders of Cynic philosophy.*

Most alarmingly, a growing number of Americans know very little about the history, nature, and importance of our unique form of government. Unaware, for example, that there is sound reason why our United States Pledge of Allegiance refers to our country as a *Republic* and why our Declaration of Independence and Constitution do not mention the word *democracy*.

Our country's founders were very aware of the failures of prior democracies, such as ancient Athens and Rome. They feared creating a government having too many similarities to a *pure democracy.* They especially recognized the importance of ensuring the right of political dissent and protecting minority groups and individuals from the *tyranny of the majority.* They knew that a *pure democracy* could result in *mob rule,* where fifty-one percent of the people could take away the rights of the other forty-nine. Through their experience, insight, and great wisdom, they put in place a one-of-its-kind *constitutional republic* — **not** a *pure democracy.*

In so doing they passed to us a very special form of government where sovereignty deliberately rests with *we the people.* Where we may act on our own or through our elected representatives to deal with issues, where our government is a servant of its people — *where our government's power comes from and is limited by its citizens.* That is, until we further screw-it-up by irresponsibly continuing to give up our U.S. citizens' Constitution-guaranteed power to an ever-growing government loaded with self-serving, self-perpetuating, power and influence craving officials!

Our *Constitutional Republic* does include some likeness to a *democracy,* such as our use of democratic processes to elect our representatives, pass new laws, etc. But, as opposed to a democracy, our U.S. Constitution *limits* our government's power and spells out how our government is to be structured. As a result, our Constitutional Republic is divided into three separate but equal branches of government. The <u>Executive</u> (*Presidency*), <u>Legislative</u> (*Congress*), and <u>Judicial</u> (*Courts*). Our Constitution establishes that no branch has absolute power, therefore providing special checks and balances on our government system and protection for the rule of law.

Our Constitution is the life-blood of our Constitutional Republic. The foundation of this land of unequaled opportunity; best hope for mankind; and envy of countless people yet deprived of and seeking liberty. A liberty for which much sacrifice has been made by so many, and for which limitless measures must always be taken to defend, protect, and preserve!

Therefore, when seeking responsibility for the existence of, and resolution of, our U.S. National Debt and Unfunded Liabilities, and our nation's other ills, we ultimately need look no further than ourselves—"we the people."

= = =

"We may define a republic to be . . . a government which derives all its powers directly or indirectly from the great body of the people, and is administered by persons holding offices during pleasure for a limited period, or during good behavior." — James Madison (1751-1836), a U.S. Founding Father; Fourth U.S. President

"But a Constitution of Government once changed from Freedom, can never be restored. Liberty, once lost, is lost forever." — John Adams (1735-1826), a U.S. Founding Father; First U.S. Vice President; Second U.S. President

"To preserve our independence, we must not let our rulers load us with perpetual debt. We must make our election between economy and liberty, or profusion and servitude." – *Thomas Jefferson (1743-1826), a U.S. Founding Father; principal author of the Declaration of Independence; 3rd U.S. President*

"A people without a language of its own is only half a nation. A nation should guard its language more than its territories, 'tis a surer barrier and more important frontier than mountain or river." – Thomas Davis (1814-1845), Irish writer; chief organizer of the Young Ireland movement.

The "Lifespan" of Our Constitutional Republic?

> *"Pure democracies have ever been spectacles of turbulence and contention; have ever been found incompatible with personal security, or the rights of property; and have, in general, been as short in their lives as they have been violent in their deaths."*
> *— James Madison (1751-1836), 4th U.S. President*

It is important to note that the "life-cycle of a democracy" scenario included on the following page is an assertion of questionable origin. While nevertheless for years quoted and referenced by many, and long accessible in many forms through an array Internet sources and other media.

However, regardless of the scenario's origin, little open-minded consideration is needed to recognize some very unsettling similarities, between it and the dangerous path our **"Constitutional Republic"** has long been on. And any realistic comparison would find us very disturbingly somewhere around mid-point between Sequence 6 and 7. That is, a nation heavily consumed with *apathy* and dangerously deep into the even more self-destructive phase of *dependence*. Leaving *bondage* the next step in this scenario — towards loss of the precious liberty/freedom now often taken for granted and abused. A path that President Trump and constructive supporters of his "Make America Great Again" agenda are striving hard to reverse.

= = =

The Life Cycle of a Democracy

"A democracy cannot exist as a permanent form of government. It will continue until the voters discover they can vote themselves generous gifts from the public treasury. From that point on, the majority will always vote for the candidates who promise the most benefits from the public treasury. Eventually every democracy will collapse, due to loose fiscal policy, and be followed by a dictatorship. From the beginning, the greatest civilizations of the world have only lasted about 200 years, and have always progressed through the following sequence:

1. From bondage to **spiritual faith**;
2. From spiritual faith to **great courage**;
3. From courage to **liberty**;
4. From liberty to **abundance**;
5. From abundance to **complacency**;
6. From complacency to **apathy**;
7. From apathy to **dependence**;
8. From dependence back to **bondage**."

= = =

"The American Republic will endure until the day Congress discovers that it can bribe the public with the public's money."
–Alexis De Tocqueville (1805-1859), French diplomat; political scientist; historian; best known for his works "Democracy in America," "The Old Regime," and "Revolution."

Our U.S. "Bill of Rights"

"We hold these truths to be self-Evident, that all men are created equal, that they are endowed by their Creator with certain unalienable Rights, that among these are **Life, Liberty and the pursuit of Happiness**. *---That to secure these rights, Governments are instituted among Men, deriving their just powers from the consent of the governed, ..."*

— *The U.S. Declaration of Independence, 1776*

The following is a transcription of the first ten amendments to our U.S. Constitution in their original form. These first ten amendments to the Constitution were ratified December 15, 1791, and form what is known as the "Bill of Rights."

Amendment I

Congress shall make no law respecting an establishment of religion, or prohibiting the free exercise thereof; or abridging the freedom of speech, or of the press; or the right of the people peaceably to assemble, and to petition the Government for a redress of grievances.

Amendment II

A well regulated Militia, being necessary to the security of a free State, the right of the people to keep and bear Arms, shall not be infringed.

Amendment III

No Soldier shall, in time of peace be quartered in any house, without the consent of the Owner, nor in time of war, but in a manner to be prescribed by law.

Amendment IV

The right of the people to be secure in their persons, houses, papers, and effects, against unreasonable searches and seizures, shall not be violated, and no Warrants shall issue, but upon probable cause, supported by Oath or affirmation, and particularly describing the place to be searched, and the persons or things to be seized.

Amendment V

No person shall be held to answer for a capital, or otherwise infamous crime, unless on a presentment or indictment of a Grand Jury, except in cases arising in the land or naval forces, or in the Militia, when in actual service in time of War or public danger; nor shall any person be subject for the same offence to be twice put in jeopardy of life or limb; nor shall be compelled in any criminal case to be a witness against himself, nor be deprived of life, liberty, or property, without due process of law; nor shall private property be taken for public use, without just compensation.

Amendment VI

In all criminal prosecutions, the accused shall enjoy the right to a speedy and public trial, by an impartial jury of the State and district wherein the crime shall have been committed, which district shall have been previously ascertained by law, and to be informed of the nature and cause of the accusation; to be confronted with the witnesses against him; to have compulsory process for obtaining witnesses in his favor, and to have the Assistance of Counsel for his defense.

Amendment VII

In Suits at common law, where the value in controversy shall exceed twenty dollars, the right of trial by jury shall be preserved, and no fact tried by a jury, shall be otherwise re-examined in any Court of the United States, than according to the rules of the common law.

Amendment VIII

Excessive bail shall not be required, nor excessive fines imposed, nor cruel and unusual punishments inflicted.

Amendment IX

The enumeration in the Constitution, of certain rights, shall not be construed to deny or disparage others retained by the people.

Amendment X

The powers not delegated to the United States by the Constitution, nor prohibited by it to the States, are reserved to the States respectively, or to the people.

= = =

"Liberty must at all hazards be supported. We have a right to it, derived from our Maker. But if we had not, our fathers have earned it for us, at the expense of their ease, their estates, their pleasure, and their blood." — *John Adams (1735-1826), a U.S. Founding Father; First U.S. Vice President; Second U.S. President*

"A Bill of Rights is what the people are entitled to against every government, and what no just government should refuse, or rest on inference." — *Thomas Jefferson (1743-1826), a U.S. Founding Father; principal author of the Declaration of Independence; 3rd U.S. President*

"The Bill of Rights wasn't enacted to give us any rights. It was enacted so the Government could not take away from us any rights that we already had." — *Kenneth Eade (1957-), an American environmental and political activist; author.*

"The Framers of the Bill of Rights did not purport to "create" rights. Rather, they designed the Bill of Rights to prohibit our Government from infringing rights and liberties presumed to be preexisting." — *William J. Brennan, Jr. (1906-1997), an Associate Justice of U.S. Supreme Court from 1956-1990.*

"Can any of you seriously say the Bill of Rights could get through Congress today? It wouldn't even get out of committee." — *F. Lee Bailey (1933-), an American former criminal defense attorney.*

Our U.S. "Pledge of Allegiance"

Official versions
(changes in __bold underline__)

1892 (first version)
"I pledge allegiance to my Flag and the republic for which it stands, one nation indivisible, with liberty and justice for all."

1892 to 1922
"I pledge allegiance to my Flag and __to__ the republic for which it stands: one nation indivisible, with liberty and justice for all."

1923
"I pledge allegiance to __the__ Flag __of the United States__ and to the republic for which it stands; one Nation indivisible with liberty and justice for all."

1924 to 1954
"I pledge allegiance to the Flag of the United States __of America__, and to the republic for which it stands; one Nation indivisible with liberty and justice for all."

1954 (current version)
"I pledge allegiance to the Flag of the United States of America, and to the Republic for which it stands, one Nation __under God,__ indivisible, with liberty and justice for all."

Section 4 of the U.S. Flag Code states in part that The Pledge of Allegiance to the Flag should ". . . be rendered by standing at attention facing the flag with the right hand over the heart. When not in uniform men should remove any non-religious headdress with their right hand and hold it at the left shoulder, the hand being over the heart. Persons in uniform should remain silent, face the flag, and render the military salute."

A Brief History of our "Pledge of Allegiance"

As shown on the previous page, the "original" **Pledge of Allegiance** read *"I pledge allegiance to my Flag and the Republic for which it stands- one nation indivisible- with liberty and justice for all."* Words written by Francis Bellamy, for Boston, Massachusetts based magazine, *The Youth's Companion,* and published on September 8, 1892, to provide students something special to repeat on Columbus Day that year. After reprinted on circulars distributed to schools throughout the country, on October 12, 1892, millions of school children repeated this *Pledge of Allegiance,* thereby starting a nation-wide school-day practice. Thereafter, on June 14, 1923, at the first National Flag Conference in Washington D.C., the words "my flag" were replaced with the formally-adopted words "the Flag of the United States." Finally, in 1942, the *Pledge of Allegiance* was officially recognized by our U.S. Congress. Then, in June 1943, the Supreme Court ruled that, as protected by the free-speech clause of the First Amendment to our U.S. Constitution, school children could not be forced to salute the Flag or say the Pledge, nor be punished for not doing so. Years later, in June 1954, the words "under God" were added by an amendment. At that time, President Dwight D. Eisenhower reportedly expressed, *"In this way we are reaffirming the transcendence of religious faith in America's heritage and future; in this way we shall constantly strengthen those spiritual weapons which forever will be our country's most powerful resource in peace and war."*

= = =

And, in our "politically-correctness-gone-mad" world of today, even "suggesting" that our children participate in such patriotic acts as saluting our U.S. Flag or reciting the Pledge of Allegiance, can often result in lawsuits, recrimination, someone being "offended," as well as teachers being suspended or fired! Clearly, our country is in much need of an appropriate measure of **"patriotic-correctness"** to ensure an at least **equal-balance** with the liberty-threatening **"political-correctness"** agenda being imposed upon us.

Our U.S. National Anthem
The Star Spangled Banner
(September 20, 1814 — By Francis Scott Key)

O say can you see, by the dawn's early light,
What so proudly we hail'd at the twilight's last gleaming,
Whose broad stripes and bright stars through the perilous fight
O'er the ramparts we watch'd were so gallantly streaming?
And the rocket's red glare, the bombs bursting in air,
Gave proof through the night that our flag was still there,
O say does that star-spangled banner yet wave
O'er the land of the free and the home of the brave?

On the shore dimly seen through the mists of the deep
Where the foe's haughty host in dread silence reposes,
What is that which the breeze, o'er the towering steep,
As it fitfully blows, half conceals, half discloses?
Now it catches the gleam of the morning's first beam,
In full glory reflected now shines in the stream,
'Tis the star-spangled banner - O long may it wave
O'er the land of the free and the home of the brave!

And where is that band who so vauntingly swore,
That the havoc of war and the battle's confusion
A home and a Country should leave us no more?
Their blood has wash'd out their foul footstep's pollution.
No refuge could save the hireling and slave
From the terror of flight or the gloom of the grave,
And the star-spangled banner in triumph doth wave
O'er the land of the free and the home of the brave.

O thus be it ever when freemen shall stand
Between their lov'd home and the war's desolation!
Blest with vict'ry and peace may the heav'n rescued land
Praise the power that hath made and preserv'd us a nation!
Then conquer we must, when our cause it is just,
And this be our motto - "In God is our trust,"
And the star-spangled banner in triumph shall wave
O'er the land of the free and the home of the brave.

A Brief History of Our U.S. National Anthem
"The Star-Spangled Banner"

The lyrics to "The Star-Spangled Banner" were composed by Francis Scott Key, an American lawyer, on September 14, 1814. After he witnessed the massive overnight British bombardment of Fort McHenry in Maryland during the War of 1812. Key watched the siege while being detained on a British ship, and penned our country's famous anthem after seeing in awe that the Fort McHenry flag had survived the awesome British assault of reportedly 1,800 bombs.

After being circulated as a handbill, the lyrics were eventually published in a Baltimore newspaper on September 20, 1814, and later set to the tune of "To Anacreon in Heaven," a popular English song.

Throughout the 19th century, "The Star-Spangled Banner" was considered the national anthem by most branches of our U.S. armed forces and other groups. However, it was not until 1916, and President Woodrow Wilson's signing of an executive order, that it was officially designated as such. Then, in March 1931, Congress passed an act confirming President Wilson's presidential order, soon followed by President Hoover signing it into law on March 3, 1931.

Our tax dollars at work . . .

An "Eight-Page" List of Federal Government Agencies!

While falsely preaching "simplicity" and "efficiency" of operations, our Federal Government continues to grow its "agencies" under a broad mix of terms and titles, such as: Agencies, Bureaus, Commissions, Departments, Services, Offices, Boards, Corporations, Foundations, Administrations, Councils, Divisions, etc., etc.   A practice especially helpful in making it difficult, if not impossible, to track ultimate responsibility; accountability; and outdated or duplicated functions, etc. Being of course among the primary aims.

= = =

- Administration Office, Executive Office of the President
  - o National Commission on Fiscal Responsibility and Reform
- Administrative Conference of the United States
- Administrative Office of United States Courts
- Advocacy and Outreach Office
- African Development Foundation
- Agency for Healthcare Research and Quality
- Agency for International Development
  - o International Development Cooperation Agency
- Agency for Toxic Substances and Disease Registry
- Aging Administration
- Agricultural Marketing Service
- Agricultural Research Service
- Agriculture Department
  - o Advocacy and Outreach Office
  - o Agricultural Marketing Service
  - o Agricultural Research Service
  - o Animal and Plant Health Inspection Service
  - o Commodity Credit Corporation
  - o Cooperative State Research, Education, and Extension Service
  - o Economic Analysis Staff
  - o Economic Research Service
  - o Energy Policy and New Uses Office
  - o Farm Service Agency
  - o Federal Crop Insurance Corporation
  - o Food and Consumer Service
  - o Food and Nutrition Service
  - o Food Safety and Inspection Service
  - o Foreign Agricultural Service
  - o Forest Service
  - o Grain Inspection, Packers and Stockyards Administration
  - o Inspector General Office, Agriculture Department
  - o National Agricultural Library
  - o National Agricultural Statistics Service
  - o National Institute of Food and Agriculture
  - o Natural Resources Conservation Service
  - o Operations Office
  - o Procurement and Property Management, Office of
  - o Risk Management Agency
  - o Rural Business-Cooperative Service
  - o Rural Housing and Community Development Service
  - o Rural Housing Service
  - o Rural Telephone Bank
  - o Rural Utilities Service
  - o Transportation Office
- Air Force Department
- Air Quality National Commission
- Air Transportation Stabilization Board

- Alaska Power Administration
- Alcohol and Tobacco Tax and Trade Bureau
- Alcohol, Tobacco, Firearms, and Explosives Bureau
- American Battle Monuments Commission
- Amtrak Reform Council
- Animal and Plant Health Inspection Service
- Antitrust Division
- Antitrust Modernization Commission
- Appalachian Regional Commission
- Appalachian States Low-Level Radioactive Waste Commission
- Architect of the Capitol
- Architectural and Transportation Barriers Compliance Board
- Arctic Research Commission
- Armed Forces Retirement Home
- Arms Control and Disarmament Agency
- Army Department
- Assassination Records Review Board
- Barry M. Goldwater Scholarship and Excellence in Education Foundation
- Bipartisan Commission on Entitlement and Tax Reform
- Board of Directors of the Hope for Homeowners Program
- Bonneville Power Administration
- Broadcasting Board of Governors
- Bureau of the Fiscal Service
- Census Bureau
- Census Monitoring Board
- Centers for Disease Control and Prevention
- Centers for Medicare & Medicaid Services
- Central Intelligence Agency
- Chemical Safety and Hazard Investigation Board
- Child Support Enforcement Office
- Children and Families Administration
- Christopher Columbus Quincentenary Jubilee Commission
- Civil Rights Commission
- Coast Guard
- Commerce Department
  - o Census Bureau
  - o Economic Analysis Bureau
  - o Economic Development Administration
  - o Economics and Statistics Administration
  - o Export Administration Bureau
  - o Foreign-Trade Zones Board
  - o Industry and Security Bureau
  - o International Trade Administration
  - o Minority Business Development Agency
  - o National Institute of Standards and Technology
  - o National Oceanic and Atmospheric Administration
  - o National Shipping Authority
  - o National Technical Information Service
  - o National Telecommunications and Information Administration
  - o Patent and Trademark Office
  - o Technology Administration
  - o Travel and Tourism Administration
- Commercial Space Transportation Office
- Commission of Fine Arts
- Commission on Immigration Reform
- Commission on Protecting and Reducing Government Secrecy
- Commission on Review of Overseas Military Facility Structure of the United States
- Commission on Structural Alternatives for the Federal Courts of Appeals
- Commission on the Advancement of Federal Law Enforcement
- Commission on the Bicentennial of the United States Constitution
- Commission on the Future of the United States Aerospace Industry
- Commission on the Social Security Notch Issue
- Committee for Purchase From People Who Are Blind or Severely Disabled
- Committee for the Implementation of Textile Agreements
- Commodity Credit Corporation
- Commodity Futures Trading Commission
- Community Development Financial Institutions Fund
- Community Living Administration
- Competitiveness Policy Council
- Comptroller of the Currency
- Congressional Budget Office
- Consumer Financial Protection Bureau
- Consumer Product Safety Commission
- Cooperative State Research, Education, and Extension Service
- Coordinating Council on Juvenile Justice and Delinquency Prevention
- Copyright Office, Library of Congress

- Copyright Royalty Board
- Copyright Royalty Judges, Library of Congress
- Corporation for National and Community Service
- Council of the Inspectors General on Integrity and Efficiency
- Council on Environmental Quality
- Counsel to the President
- Court Services and Offender Supervision Agency for the District of Columbia
- Crime and Security in U.S. Seaports, Interagency Commission
- Customs Service

- Defense Acquisition Regulations System
- Defense Base Closure and Realignment Commission
- Defense Contract Audit Agency
- Defense Criminal Investigative Service
- Defense Department
  - o Air Force Department
  - o Army Department
  - o Defense Acquisition Regulations System
  - o Defense Contract Audit Agency
  - o Defense Criminal Investigative Service
  - o Defense Information Systems Agency
  - o Defense Intelligence Agency
  - o Defense Investigative Service
  - o Defense Logistics Agency
  - o Defense Mapping Agency
  - o Defense Special Weapons Agency
  - o Engineers Corps
  - o National Geospatial-Intelligence Agency
  - o National Security Agency/Central Security Service
  - o Navy Department
  - o Uniformed Services University of the Health Sciences
- Defense Information Systems Agency
- Defense Intelligence Agency
- Defense Investigative Service
- Defense Logistics Agency
- Defense Mapping Agency
- Defense Nuclear Facilities Safety Board
- Defense Special Weapons Agency
- Delaware River Basin Commission
- Denali Commission
- Disability Employment Policy Office
- Drug Enforcement Administration
- Economic Analysis Bureau
- Economic Analysis Staff
- Economic Development Administration
- Economic Research Service
- Economics and Statistics Administration
- Education Department
- Election Assistance Commission
- Electronic Commerce Advisory Commission
- Emergency Oil and Gas Guaranteed Loan Board
- Emergency Steel Guarantee Loan Board
- Employee Benefits Security Administration
- Employees Compensation Appeals Board
- Employment and Training Administration
- Employment Standards Administration
- Energy Department
  - o Alaska Power Administration
  - o Bonneville Power Administration
  - o Energy Efficiency and Renewable Energy Office
  - o Energy Information Administration
  - o Energy Research Office
  - o Environment Office, Energy Department
  - o Federal Energy Regulatory Commission
  - o Hearings and Appeals Office, Energy Department
  - o Minority Economic Impact Office
  - o National Nuclear Security Administration
  - o Nuclear Energy Office
  - o Southeastern Power Administration
  - o Southwestern Power Administration
  - o Western Area Power Administration
- Energy Efficiency and Renewable Energy Office
- Energy Information Administration
- Energy Policy and New Uses Office
- Energy Research Office
- Engineers Corps
- Engraving and Printing Bureau
- Environment Office, Energy Department
- Environmental Protection Agency
- Equal Employment Opportunity Commission
- Executive Council on Integrity and Efficiency
- Executive Office for Immigration Review
- Executive Office of the President
  - o Administration Office, Executive Office of the President
  - o Council on Environmental Quality
  - o Counsel to the President
- Export Administration Bureau
- Export-Import Bank
- Family Assistance Office
- Farm Credit Administration
- Farm Credit System Insurance Corporation
- Farm Service Agency
- Federal Accounting Standards Advisory Board
- Federal Acquisition Regulation System
- Federal Aviation Administration
- Federal Bureau of Investigation

- Federal Communications Commission
- Federal Contract Compliance Programs Office
- Federal Crop Insurance Corporation
- Federal Deposit Insurance Corporation
- Federal Election Commission
- Federal Emergency Management Agency
- Federal Energy Regulatory Commission
- Federal Financial Institutions Examination Council
- Federal Highway Administration
- Federal Housing Enterprise Oversight Office
- Federal Housing Finance Agency
- Federal Housing Finance Board
- Federal Labor Relations Authority
  - o Federal Service Impasses Panel
- Federal Law Enforcement Training Center
- Federal Maritime Commission
- Federal Mediation and Conciliation Service
- Federal Mine Safety and Health Review Commission
- Federal Motor Carrier Safety Administration
- Federal Pay, Advisory Committee
- Federal Prison Industries
- Federal Procurement Policy Office
- Federal Railroad Administration
- Federal Register Office
- Federal Register, Administrative Committee
- Federal Reserve System
- Federal Retirement Thrift Investment Board
- Federal Service Impasses Panel
- Federal Trade Commission
- Federal Transit Administration
- Financial Crimes Enforcement Network
- Financial Crisis Inquiry Commission
- Financial Research Office
- Financial Stability Oversight Council
- First Responder Network Authority
- Fiscal Service
- Fish and Wildlife Service
- Food and Consumer Service
- Food and Drug Administration
- Food and Nutrition Service
- Food Safety and Inspection Service
- Foreign Agricultural Service
- Foreign Assets Control Office
- Foreign Claims Settlement Commission
- Foreign Service Grievance Board
- Foreign Service Impasse Disputes Panel
- Foreign Service Labor Relations Board
- Foreign-Trade Zones Board
- Forest Service
- General Services Administration
- Geographic Names Board
- Geological Survey
- Government Accountability Office
- Government Ethics Office
- Government National Mortgage Association
- Government Publishing Office
- Grain Inspection, Packers and Stockyards Administration
- Gulf Coast Ecosystem Restoration Council
- Harry S. Truman Scholarship Foundation
- Health and Human Services Department
  - o Agency for Healthcare Research and Quality
  - o Agency for Toxic Substances and Disease Registry
  - o Aging Administration
  - o Centers for Disease Control and Prevention
  - o Centers for Medicare & Medicaid Services
  - o Child Support Enforcement Office
  - o Children and Families Administration
  - o Community Living Administration
  - o Family Assistance Office
  - o Food and Drug Administration
  - o Health Care Finance Administration
  - o Health Resources and Services Administration
  - o Indian Health Service
  - o Inspector General Office, Health and Human Services Department
  - o National Institutes of Health
  - o National Library of Medicine
  - o Program Support Center
  - o Public Health Service
  - o Refugee Resettlement Office
  - o Substance Abuse and Mental Health Services Administration
- Health Care Finance Administration
- Health Resources and Services Administration
- Hearings and Appeals Office, Energy Department
- Hearings and Appeals Office, Interior Department
- Historic Preservation, Advisory Council
- Homeland Security Department

- o Coast Guard
- o Federal Emergency Management Agency
- o Federal Law Enforcement Training Center
- o National Communications System
- o Secret Service
- o Transportation Security Administration
- o U.S. Citizenship and Immigration Services
- o U.S. Customs and Border Protection
- o U.S. Immigration and Customs Enforcement
- • Housing and Urban Development Department
- o Federal Housing Enterprise Oversight Office
- o Government National Mortgage Association
- • Immigration and Naturalization Service
- • Indian Affairs Bureau
- • Indian Arts and Crafts Board
- • Indian Health Service
- • Indian Trust Transition Office
- • Industry and Security Bureau
- • Information Security Oversight Office
- • Inspector General Office, Agriculture Department
- • Inspector General Office, Health and Human Services Department
- • Institute of American Indian and Alaska Native Culture and Arts Development
- • Institute of Museum and Library Services
- • Inter-American Foundation
- • Interagency Floodplain Management Review Committee
- • Intergovernmental Relations Advisory Commission
- • Interior Department
- o Fish and Wildlife Service
- o Geological Survey
- o Hearings and Appeals Office, Interior Department
- o Indian Affairs Bureau
- o Indian Trust Transition Office
- o Land Management Bureau
- o Minerals Management Service
- o Mines Bureau
- o National Biological Service
- o National Civilian Community Corps
- o National Indian Gaming Commission
- o National Park Service
- o Natural Resources Revenue Office
- o Ocean Energy Management Bureau
- o Ocean Energy Management, Regulation, and Enforcement Bureau
- o Reclamation Bureau
- o Safety and Environmental Enforcement Bureau
- o Special Trustee for American Indians Office
- o Surface Mining Reclamation and Enforcement Office
- • Internal Revenue Service
- • International Boundary and Water Commission, United States and Mexico
- • International Broadcasting Board
- • International Development Cooperation Agency
- • International Investment Office
- • International Joint Commission-United States and Canada
- • International Organizations Employees Loyalty Board
- • International Trade Administration
- • International Trade Commission
- • Interstate Commerce Commission
- • James Madison Memorial Fellowship Foundation
- • Japan-United States Friendship Commission
- • Joint Board for Enrollment of Actuaries
- • Judicial Conference of the United States
- • Judicial Review Commission on Foreign Asset Control
- • Justice Department
- o Alcohol, Tobacco, Firearms, and Explosives Bureau
- o Antitrust Division
- o Drug Enforcement Administration
- o Executive Office for Immigration Review
- o Federal Bureau of Investigation
- o Federal Prison Industries
- o Foreign Claims Settlement Commission
- o Immigration and Naturalization Service
- o Justice Programs Office
- o Juvenile Justice and Delinquency Prevention Office
- o National Institute of Corrections
- o National Institute of Justice
- o Parole Commission
- o Prisons Bureau
- o United States Marshals Service
- • Justice Programs Office
- o Victims of Crime Office
- • Juvenile Justice and Delinquency Prevention Office
- • Labor Department
- o Disability Employment Policy Office
- o Employee Benefits Security Administration
- o Employees Compensation Appeals Board
- o Employment and Training Administration
- o Employment Standards Administration

- o Federal Contract Compliance Programs Office
- o Labor Statistics Bureau
- o Labor-Management Standards Office
- o Mine Safety and Health Administration
- o Occupational Safety and Health Administration
- o Pension and Welfare Benefits Administration
- o Veterans Employment and Training Service
- o Wage and Hour Division
- o Workers Compensation Programs Office
  - • Labor Statistics Bureau
  - • Labor-Management Standards Office
  - • Land Management Bureau
  - • Legal Services Corporation
  - • Library of Congress
- o Copyright Office, Library of Congress
- o Copyright Royalty Board
  - • Local Television Loan Guarantee Board
  - • Management and Budget Office
- o Federal Procurement Policy Office
  - • Marine Mammal Commission
  - • Maritime Administration
  - • Medicare Payment Advisory Commission
  - • Merit Systems Protection Board
  - • Military Compensation and Retirement Modernization Commission
  - • Millennium Challenge Corporation
  - • Mine Safety and Health Administration
  - • Minerals Management Service
  - • Mines Bureau
  - • Minority Business Development Agency
  - • Minority Economic Impact Office
  - • Mississippi River Commission
  - • Monetary Offices
  - • Morris K. Udall and Stewart L. Udall Foundation
  - • National Aeronautics and Space Administration
  - • National Agricultural Library
  - • National Agricultural Statistics Service
  - • National Archives and Records Administration
- o Federal Register Office
- o Information Security Oversight Office
- o National Historical Publications and Records Commission
  - • National Bankruptcy Review Commission
  - • National Biological Service
  - • National Bipartisan Commission on Future of Medicare
  - • National Capital Planning Commission
  - • National Civilian Community Corps
  - • National Commission on Fiscal Responsibility and Reform
  - • National Commission on Intermodal Transportation
  - • National Commission on Libraries and Information Science
  - • National Commission on Manufactured Housing
  - • National Commission on Terrorist Attacks Upon the United States
  - • National Commission on the Cost of Higher Education
  - • National Communications System
  - • National Consumer Cooperative Bank
  - • National Council on Disability
  - • National Counterintelligence Center
  - • National Credit Union Administration
  - • National Crime Prevention and Privacy Compact Council
  - • National Economic Council
  - • National Education Goals Panel
  - • National Endowment for the Arts
  - • National Endowment for the Humanities
  - • National Foundation on the Arts and the Humanities
- o Institute of Museum and Library Services
- o National Endowment for the Arts
- o National Endowment for the Humanities
  - • National Gambling Impact Study Commission
  - • National Geospatial-Intelligence Agency
  - • National Highway Traffic Safety Administration
  - • National Historical Publications and Records Commission
  - • National Indian Gaming Commission
  - • National Institute for Literacy
  - • National Institute of Corrections
  - • National Institute of Food and Agriculture
  - • National Institute of Justice
  - • National Institute of Standards and Technology
  - • National Institutes of Health
  - • National Intelligence, Office of the National Director
  - • National Labor Relations Board
  - • National Library of Medicine
  - • National Mediation Board
  - • National Nanotechnology Coordination Office
  - • National Nuclear Security Administration
  - • National Oceanic and Atmospheric Administration
  - • National Park Service
  - • National Partnership for Reinventing Government
  - • National Prison Rape Elimination Commission

- National Railroad Passenger Corporation
- National Science Foundation
- National Security Agency/Central Security Service
- National Security Council
- National Shipping Authority
- National Skill Standards Board
- National Technical Information Service
- National Telecommunications and Information Administration
  - o First Responder Network Authority
- National Transportation Safety Board
- National Women's Business Council
- Natural Resources Conservation Service
- Natural Resources Revenue Office
- Navajo and Hopi Indian Relocation Office
- Navy Department
- Neighborhood Reinvestment Corporation
- Northeast Dairy Compact Commission
- Northeast Interstate Low-Level Radioactive Waste Commission
- Nuclear Energy Office
- Nuclear Regulatory Commission
- Nuclear Waste Technical Review Board
- Occupational Safety and Health Administration
- Occupational Safety and Health Review Commission
- Ocean Energy Management Bureau
- Ocean Energy Management, Regulation, and Enforcement Bureau
- Ocean Policy Commission
- Office of Motor Carrier Safety
- Office of National Drug Control Policy
- Office of Policy Development
- Oklahoma City National Memorial Trust
- Operations Office
- Ounce of Prevention Council
- Overseas Private Investment Corporation
- Pacific Northwest Electric Power and Conservation Planning Council
- Panama Canal Commission
- Parole Commission
- Patent and Trademark Office
- Peace Corps
- Pension and Welfare Benefits Administration
- Pension Benefit Guaranty Corporation
- Personnel Management Office
- Physician Payment Review Commission
- Pipeline and Hazardous Materials Safety Administration
- Postal Rate Commission
- Postal Regulatory Commission
- Postal Service
- President's Council on Integrity and Efficiency
- President's Council on Sustainable Development
- President's Critical Infrastructure Protection Board
- President's Economic Policy Advisory Board
- Presidential Advisory Committee on Gulf War Veterans' Illnesses
- Presidential Commission on Assignment of Women in the Armed Forces
- Presidential Documents
- Presidio Trust
- Prisons Bureau
- Privacy and Civil Liberties Oversight Board
- Procurement and Property Management, Office of
- Program Support Center
- Prospective Payment Assessment Commission
- Public Debt Bureau
- Public Health Service
- Railroad Retirement Board
- Reagan-Udall Foundation for the Food and Drug Administration
- Reclamation Bureau
- Recovery Accountability and Transparency Board
- Refugee Resettlement Office
- Regulatory Information Service Center
- Research and Innovative Technology Administration
- Research and Special Programs Administration
- Resolution Trust Corporation
- Risk Management Agency
- Rural Business-Cooperative Service
- Rural Housing and Community Development Service
- Rural Housing Service
- Rural Telephone Bank
- Rural Utilities Service
- Safety and Environmental Enforcement Bureau
- Saint Lawrence Seaway Development Corporation
- Science and Technology Policy Office
- Secret Service
- Securities and Exchange Commission
- Selective Service System
- Small Business Administration
- Smithsonian Institution
- Social Security Administration
- Southeastern Power Administration

- Southwestern Power Administration
- Special Counsel Office
- Special Inspector General for Afghanistan Reconstruction
- Special Inspector General For Iraq Reconstruction
- Special Trustee for American Indians Office
- State Department
- State Justice Institute
- Substance Abuse and Mental Health Services Administration
- Surface Mining Reclamation and Enforcement Office
- Surface Transportation Board
- Susquehanna River Basin Commission
- Technology Administration
- Tennessee Valley Authority
- The White House Office
- Thrift Depositor Protection Oversight Board
- Thrift Supervision Office
- Trade and Development Agency
- Trade Representative, Office of United States
- Transportation Department
  - Commercial Space Transportation Office
  - Federal Aviation Administration
  - Federal Highway Administration
  - Federal Motor Carrier Safety Administration
  - Federal Railroad Administration
  - Federal Transit Administration
  - Maritime Administration
  - National Highway Traffic Safety Administration
  - Office of Motor Carrier Safety
  - Pipeline and Hazardous Materials Safety Administration
  - Research and Innovative Technology Administration
  - Research and Special Programs Administration
  - Saint Lawrence Seaway Development Corporation
  - Surface Transportation Board
  - Transportation Statistics Bureau
- Transportation Office
- Transportation Security Administration
- Transportation Statistics Bureau
- Travel and Tourism Administration
- Treasury Department
  - Alcohol and Tobacco Tax and Trade Bureau
  - Bureau of the Fiscal Service
  - Community Development Financial Institutions Fund
  - Comptroller of the Currency
  - Customs Service
  - Engraving and Printing Bureau
  - Financial Crimes Enforcement Network
  - Financial Research Office
  - Fiscal Service
  - Foreign Assets Control Office
  - Internal Revenue Service
  - International Investment Office
  - Monetary Offices
  - Public Debt Bureau
  - Thrift Supervision Office
  - United States Mint
- Twenty-First Century Workforce Commission
- U.S. Citizenship and Immigration Services
- U.S. Customs and Border Protection
- U.S. House of Representatives
- U.S. Immigration and Customs Enforcement
- U.S. Trade Deficit Review Commission
- U.S.-China Economic and Security Review Commission
- Uniformed Services University of the Health Sciences
- United States Enrichment Corporation
- United States Information Agency
- United States Institute of Peace
- United States Marshals Service
- United States Mint
- United States Sentencing Commission
- Utah Reclamation Mitigation and Conservation Commission
- Valles Caldera Trust
- Veterans Affairs Department
- Veterans Employment and Training Service
- Victims of Crime Office
- Wage and Hour Division
- Western Area Power Administration
- Women's Business Enterprise Interagency Committee
- Women's Progress Commemoration Commission
- Workers Compensation Programs Office

"As government expands, liberty contracts."

— Ronald Reagan (1911-2004), 40th U.S. President.

References & Recommended Reading
(Listed Alphabetically by Author's Last Name)

Book Title	Author
The Torah; Holy Bible; Qur'an (Koran); and/or Other Religious Text of one's respective Faith or otherwise interest. *[Listed in chronological order.]*	(Most literal translation and reader-friendly format of choice.)
Crisis Of Character	Gary J. Byrne
The Debt Bomb	Senator Tom Coburn & John Hart
There Goes My Social Life: From Clueless to Conservative	Stacey Dash
Hillary's America	Dinesh D'Souza
Clinton Cash	Chuck Dixon; Brett R. Smith; Peter Schweizer
All I Really Need To Know I Learned In Kindergarten	Robert Fulghum
• Because They Hate • They Must Be Stopped: Why We Must Defeat Radical Islam and How We Can Do It	Brigitte Gabriel
The Haldeman Diaries – Inside The Nixon White House	H. R. Haldeman (Introduction and Afterword by Stephen E. Ambrose)
The Federalist Papers	Alexander Hamilton, James Madison, & John Jay (Introduction by Gary Wills)
See Something, Say Nothing: A Homeland Security Officer Exposes the Government's Submission to Jihad	Philip Haney & Art Moore

References & Recommended Reading – *(Continued)*
(Listed Alphabetically by Author's Last Name)

Book Title	Author
Hostile Waters	Peter Huchthausen, Igor Kurdin, & R. Alan White
White House Burning	Simon Johnson James Kwak
Who Moved My Cheese?	Spencer Johnson
Two Incomes and Still Broke?	Linda Kelley
The Imitation Of Christ	Thomas A. Kempis
Lights Out	Ted Koppel
Trump Revealed	Michael Kranish; Mark Fisher
• The Liberty Amendments • Plunder and Deceit • Ameritopia • Liberty and Tyranny	Mark R. Levin
The Patriot's Reference	Edited by: Joel J. Miller & Kristen Parrish
Armageddon	Dick Morris; Eileen McGann
• Threats To Our Liberty & Survival • Killing "Life, Liberty, & Pursuit of Happiness • Destruction From Within • "Our" U.S. National Debt – 101 • A Pandemic of Lunacy	William James Moore

References & Recommended Reading – *(Continued)*
(Listed Alphabetically by Author's Last Name)

Book Title	Author
• Killing Jesus • Killing Lincoln • Killing Patton • Killing Kennedy	Bill O'Reilly
I'm Not OK. You're Not OK. But It's OK!	Chris Padgett
Words That Inspired Him— A Lifetime Of Favorite Writings, Poems & Quotations	Norman Vincent Peal
The Most of Andy Rooney *(ESP Article: "Mr. Rooney goes to Washington")*	Andrew A. Rooney
• Liberalism Is A Mental Disorder • Stop The Coming Civil War • Countdown To Mecca • Government Zero • Scorched Earth • God, Faith, & Reason • Stop Mass Hysteria	Michael Savage
The Faith Explained	Leo J. Trese
• The Art of the Deal • Great Again	Donald J. Trump; Tony Schwartz Donald J. Trump
Enemies—A History of the FBI	Tim Weiner
• Mutterings Of An Old Man • I Felt The Floor Shake	Mike Womeldorff
• House Calls • Office Calls • Love Letters from a Marriage • Wisdom for a Woman • Wisdom for a Man	Gary Yarbrough, M.D.

References & Recommended Reading – *(Continued)*
(Random Listing)

Internet Link Title	Internet Address
U.S. National Debt Clock : Real Time	http://www.usdebtclock.org/
What Is National Debt?	https://www.thoughtco.com/definition-of-national-debt-1146136
The National Debt, Explained	http://theweek.com/articles/747998/national-debt-explained
How Big Is A Trillion Dollars In Singles? A Comparison	http://geekologie.com/2018/03/how-big-is-a-trillion-dollars-in-singles.php
United States GDP: 1960--2018	https://tradingeconomics.com/united-states/gdp
Treasury Direct: The Debt To The Penny And Who Holds It	https://www.treasurydirect.gov/NP/debt/current
Treasury Direct: Interest Expense On The Debt Outstanding	https://www.treasurydirect.gov/gov't/reports/ir/ir_expense.htm
Office of Management and Budget: Budget and Spending	https://www.whitehouse.gov/issues/budget-spending/
Office of Management and Budget: Historical Tables	https://www.whitehouse.gov/omb/historical-tables/
Congressional Budget Office: Federal Debt and Interest Costs	https://www.cbo.gov/publication/21960
Central Intelligence Agency (CIA): The World Fact Book	https://www.cia.gov/library/publications/the-world-factbook/

"Enjoy the Little Things"

> "Enjoy the little things, for one day you may look back and realize they were the big things." — Robert Brault (1963-), American operatic tenor; author.

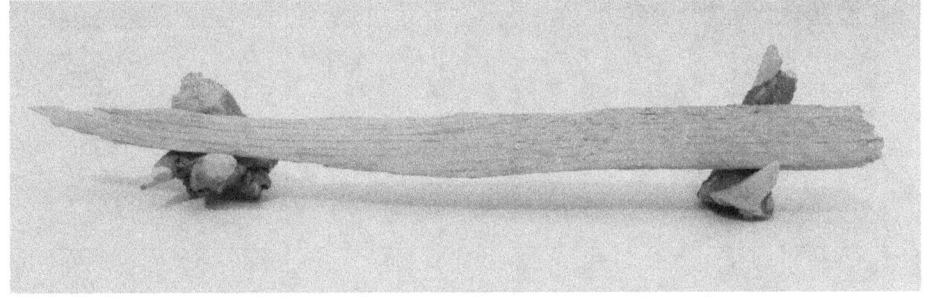

Hand-carvings by Matthew, 2011

"As you admire the wonderful things God has made today, remember you're one of them, wonderful inside and out. You are blessed, you are special, you are loved." –Author Unknown

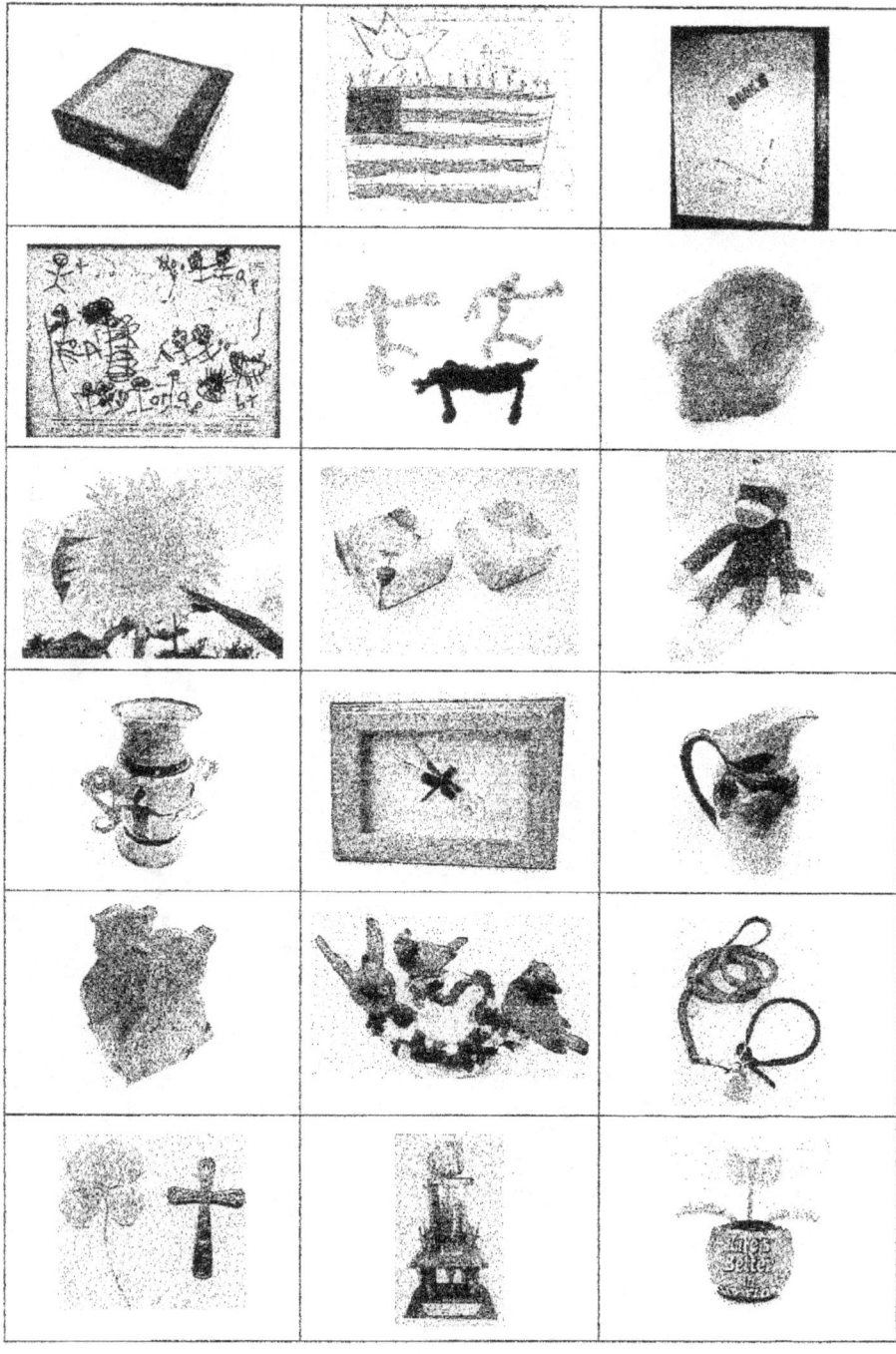

*"**Risk** more than others think is safe. **Care** more than others think is wise. **Dream** more than others think is practical. **Expect** more than others think is possible."* –Claude Bissell (1916-2000), Canadian author; educator.

"It's not about time, it's about choices. How are you spending your choices?" — Beverly Adamo

"He who hunts for flowers will find flowers; and he who loves weeds will find weeds." — Henry Ward Beecher

"Never despair, but if you do, work on in despair."
— Edmund Burke

"Fear knocked at the door. Faith answered.
And lo, no one was there."
— Anonymous